This book is not the illusive
it a manual for those wanti
search in vain for platitude
Rather, like C. S. Lewis's *A*                                        n
honest autobiography to (.
tangible shadow that depression casts. With understanding
compassion, Mark Meynell undergirds the sufferer with a
confidence in the Lord, who sometimes appears to work against
himself in our lives. It is compelling yet practical reading, written
with integrity, warmth and trust in Christ, who is the High Priest
in touch with our reality. All who read this will feel deeply
indebted to Mark Meynell, and to God who has taught him
so much in the blizzard of suffering.
*Roger Carswell, evangelist and author*

A moving and fascinating description of the life of a preacher
battling depression. Mark writes openly and honestly about
his 'black dog', and in doing so is able expertly to explain the
importance of God's grace in breaking the depressive feelings of
guilt, abuse, abandonment and betrayal. This book offers a light
at the end of the tunnel, whether you're a sufferer or supporter.
*Sean Fletcher, broadcaster*

What makes this book on depression stand out from a crowded
field is the mixture of fine writing, personal honesty, intellectual
analysis, theological incisiveness and simple open-endedness:
Mark does not proffer a cure, but he does offer you a walking
companion for the dark journey. And anyone who has a friend
with depression will find it even more helpful. So, all in all, it's
a must-buy and a must-read.
*Julian Hardyman, Senior Pastor, Eden Baptist Church, Cambridge*

A poignant and powerful description of one man's continuing
journey to understand and manage depression. Mark Meynell's
eloquent book is written straight from the heart of pain – yet it
is brimful of hope and courage, and will help anyone whose life
has been touched by mental illness. Meynell is defiantly not
defined by his afflictions, which are only one part of the life of
this exceptional man, minister and writer. In finding the courage

to pen this important book, Meynell has illuminated not just his own experience, but will help many others to make sense of their own lives. He has certainly helped me to make more sense of mine.

*Rachel Kelly, author of the* Sunday Times *top ten bestseller* Black Rainbow: How Words Healed Me – My Journey Through Depression, *and ambassador for SANE and Rethink Mental Illness*

A thoughtful and courageous book, which reflects on what it means to live as a Christian with depression. Writing from experience, Mark navigates us through the darkness of despair, and shines gospel light on issues such as shame, guilt and fear. As we journey with him, we are reminded that we are not alone – and pointed to a Saviour who brings us purpose, grace and hope.

*Emma Scrivener, author, blogger and speaker*

As a fellow-sufferer, albeit one who has not suffered quite as severely, I welcome Mark Meynell's courageous book. It is full of raw honesty, and powerfully articulates the struggles and confusions which depression throws up, especially to those in Christian ministry who, whatever the pretence, are not insulated from it. At the same time, it offers practical wisdom and hope to those who struggle, without being trite. I'd recommend it to all who suffer, for them to read slowly and gently. I'd also recommend it to those seeking to care for someone with depression, or understand its nature and how a sufferer can continue to serve Christ well through weakness.

*Derek Tidball, author, Bible teacher and former Principal of London School of Theology*

In this profound, unusual and very personal book, Mark Meynell reflects on living with the painful thorn in the flesh of a vulnerability to depression, and how that has affected his view of himself and the reactions of those around him as he seeks to pastor and teach while openly admitting his struggle. He touches on many difficult subjects – the causes of depression, wrestling with suicidal thoughts, why God allows suffering, shame and guilt, what not to say to people who are depressed . . . and overall he demonstrates the extraordinary relevance and power of the

Bible in helping us to connect our often mysterious and confusing experiences to God's bigger story. But no trite or easy answers here. His creative appendix of music, books, poetry, and websites and blogs that have helped him survive his 'cave' of depression is invaluable.

*Richard Winter, Professor Emeritus of Counselling, Covenant Seminary, St Louis, USA*

Mark's empathy as a friend, his gentle love for Jesus as a pastor, provides us with wise guidance and that rarest of care that helps us feel that we are known and accepted. Mark does not write as one who has arrived. The hope he offers is neither trite nor cruel. Instead, he invites us fellow cave-dwellers and those who love us to walk (or collapse) with him on the road. Jesus kisses us and holds us there. He fights on our behalf there. Guilt and shame are no match for him. They run in fear and let us alone. For the first time in a long while, we rest.

*Zack Eswine, Pastor, Riverside Church, and Director of Homiletics, Covenant Theological Seminary, St Louis, Missouri*

MARK
MEYNELL
WHEN
DARKNESS
SEEMS
MY
CLOSEST
FRIEND

# MARK MEYNELL

# WHEN DARKNESS SEEMS MY CLOSEST FRIEND

Reflections on life and ministry with depression

INTER-VARSITY PRESS
36 Causton Street, London SW1P 4ST, England
Email: ivp@ivpbooks.com
Website: www.ivpbooks.com

*First published 2018*

**British Library Cataloguing-in-Publication Data**
A catalogue record for this book is available from the British Library.

ISBN: 978-1-78359-650-8
eBook ISBN: 978-1-78359-651-5

Set in Dante 12/15pt
Typeset in Great Britain by CRB Associates, Potterhanworth, Lincolnshire
Printed in Great Britain by Ashford Colour Press Ltd, Gosport, Hampshire

*Inter-Varsity Press publishes Christian books that are true to the Bible and that
communicate the gospel, develop discipleship and strengthen the church for its mission
in the world.*

*IVP originated within the Inter-Varsity Fellowship, now the Universities and Colleges
Christian Fellowship, a student movement connecting Christian Unions in universities
and colleges throughout Great Britain, and a member movement of the International
Fellowship of Evangelical Students. Website: www.uccf.org.uk. That historic association
is maintained, and all senior IVP staff and committee members subscribe to the UCCF
Basis of Faith.*

To my Balkan brothers

Slavko Hadzic and Kosta Milkov

More faithful friends
this cave-dweller has not found

# CONTENTS

# ACKNOWLEDGMENTS

So many people have helped me to reach this point. Never has it been clearer to me how much of a collaborative effort life is! And that's before I even got to the business of writing all this down.

My family have of course been an ever-present source of love and stability, despite my fluctuations and perplexing responses. I owe Rachel, Joshua and Zanna more than words can possibly say. Mum and Dad have also been rocks, despite all the storms that they themselves have had to weather.

Many have been my cave friends, from within and without. A handful don't want to be mentioned, which I totally understand – but you know who you are. Thank you.

I'm very fortunate to have a job that not only takes me to many parts of the world, but, more importantly, gives me the chance to build deep friendships cross-culturally. This list, thankfully, reflects that joyful privilege.

I must thank my Langham colleagues who have encouraged me with this: Chris Wright has read through, and been very encouraging of, this book. My immediate boss, Paul Windsor, has become a treasured friend and been very supportive of this project. Finally, Pieter Kwant has been a wonderful agent and encourager.

Then, thanks to these few who have been stalwart friends by helping, advising, encouraging, tweaking and sustaining the writing of this book: Ellie Bayliss, Libby Barnardo, Paul Carter (Lexington VA, USA), Jennifer Cuthbertson (Cornelius NC, USA, also a Langham colleague), Tim Davies, Louanne Enns, Andrew Fellows, Slavko Hadzic (Sarajevo, Bosnia and Herzegovina), Daniela Hagmüller (Graz, Austria), Simon Hawkins, Marcus Honeysett, George Ladas (Athens, Greece), Tanya Marlow, Gavin McGrath, Kosta Milkov (Skopje, Macedonia), Ed Moll, Trevor Pearce, Hannah Phillips (Austin TX, USA), Toni Popov (Ohrid, Macedonia), Eduardo Rojas (Cochabamba, Bolivia), Emma Scrivener. Each has improved the book in countless and immeasurable ways. So, thank you! I am also grateful to Eleanor Trotter at IVP for her support and work on the book.

Needless to say, any infelicities or unhelpful inclusions are entirely my responsibility. I can only hope that all who read this will have the grace to overlook them!

Finally, I should explain the dedication. Both Slavko and Kosta have read, and commented on, the various chapters as they have appeared, and so fully deserve their inclusion in the acknowledgments list. However, over the last decade, they have become far more than mere editorial assistants. We have had the joy of working together at various points and in various cities (I've lost count now of where and when!). They are fantastic colleagues to have. But even better than that, they have taken the time to listen and care, too often when at my lowest ebb and thousands of miles from home.

It is a cliché, but as we have served and supported each other and our families, the three of us have shared more laughter, tears and encouragements than I could have dared to expect of any friends. And, for that reason, I have no hesitation in expressing my love and gratitude to them by dedicating this to my most faithful cave friends.

*Norfolk*
*Soli Deo Gloria*

# INTRODUCTION

Rachel and I were sitting in our hotel near Entebbe airport glued to the TV while our children (then aged four and nearly seven) played. It was our last night in Uganda after almost exactly four years, and we were returning to England to live in London.

And it was 7/7.

On that terrible day in 2005, Islamist extremists bombed three tube trains and a bus, killing fifty-two and injuring over 700. As we watched the reports in impotent horror 4,000 miles away, it struck us that these atrocities seemed to form a semicircle around our new address. I had passed through each location hundreds of times. I was not present that day. Yet some friends and family were – my brother was actually sitting on the train immediately ahead of the one that exploded at King's Cross.

There was a grim irony to it all. A handful of friends had been alarmed by our move to Africa with two tiny people in tow (Zanna, our daughter, was only ten weeks old), fearing that it would be too dangerous. Of course, every continent has its no-go areas, and perhaps Africa has more than many. But we were remarkably safe in Kampala. So it was more a reflection of their lack of personal experience of the region rather than anything. Yet now, here we were preparing to return at the very moment when central London had become a war zone.

As it happened, normal flights were quickly resumed and we moved into our flat a month later. Our furniture came by sea freight and didn't arrive until late October. But, apart from that, everything went without a hitch.

Until my mind seemed to fall apart.

I had returned for a dream job – to be on the senior ministry team of All Souls, Langham Place, working again with the then newly installed Rector, Hugh Palmer (who had also been my boss when we lived in Sheffield), complete with a generous agreement of six weeks a year to work for Langham Partnership.[1] Yet I was in a bad place. Hugh kindly allowed me to delay my start, so, appropriately enough, my first day was All Souls' Day – 2nd November. We all probably assumed the issue was reverse culture shock. That was partly it, of course, but it didn't explain everything.

Eventually, I knew I needed professional help. A psychiatrist soon diagnosed me with a form of PTSD (post-traumatic stress disorder) and prescribed medication, with incrementally increasing doses over the coming weeks. PTSD is perhaps most commonly associated with military veterans returning from the battlefield. But it is not exclusive to soldiers. I was very soon prescribed quite rapidly increasing doses of medication.

I sense that mental illness resembles a bone fracture. Bones have remarkable durability, but also, once broken, can rapidly heal and be reset. With normal daily use, one might never be aware of past problems. But a healed bone may or may not be as robust as it was before the break. A vulnerability still remains, the constant potential for a repeat fracture, which is why caution is always necessary.

Depression, and indeed the whole gamut of mental illness, is so varied that generalizations are rarely helpful. It can strike at almost any age, individuals from all walks of life, temperaments and ethnicities. It is no respecter of the divisions that bedevil human society. Sometimes there are obvious causes or triggers; often, there are none at all, its roots perhaps lost in the remotest strata of our genetic inheritance. Sometimes the affliction disappears as mysteriously as it arrives. It can stop people completely in their tracks, perhaps becoming so acute that it leads to periods of hospitalization. For some, it is mercifully brief; for others, chronic, but somehow compatible with a semblance of normal working life. For me, it has been an ongoing, ever-present consciousness, a constant ache with occasional stabbing pains. I don't have great highs, though occasionally I envy the thought of them (until I remember that, for friends with the likes of bipolar disorder, these can be just as hard to navigate as the lows).

So this is not a book about a great cure, still less a wonderful deliverance. Although I do believe that will come, *in the end*. This is written while still on the journey. I write as a Christian believer, who strives to hold to what creedal Christianity has stood for over centuries. I write as a Christian minister, with the pastoral responsibilities and concerns that brings. Which is to say that I try never to duck the difficulties or pain – because that serves *nobody's* best interests. Instead, I try to be real, showing where I have struggled and, more acutely, felt like giving up.

What follows is a series of reflections on aspects of the experience – as much for my own need to figure things out as to help others to understand it better. As the English novelist

E. M. Forster once quipped, 'How do I know what I think until I see what I say?' My feelings precisely! Of course, the primary risk of figuring this out in public is that in certain quarters I now become 'the depression guy'. Yet, while I recognize that depression is my chronic reality, akin to other different afflictions that many endure, I am clear that it does not form my identity. It is *not* how I define myself. It occupies nothing like the totality of my ministry nor areas of professional interest (as my speaking and writing ought to make abundantly clear). It is merely one of many elements in the mosaic of inheritance and influence that make up my life.

If what I write helps you in some small way to know what you think, or perhaps to understand what a friend thinks, then I rejoice.

# 1. THE MASK

Nobody really knew. For that matter, I didn't really know. It was so artfully concealed that even those closest to me could only have sensed that things were a bit out of kilter. But that's all. Most probably put it down to being a more emotional or melancholy sort. 'Oh, Mark? He's OK – a bit up and down, perhaps, but basically just a typical arty type!' I always described myself as an emotional yoyo anyway.

But, in late 2005, I had to come to terms with a situation that was more serious than that. Prior to that point, I had masked it – not least, from myself.

## On the pros and cons of masks

I was one of those antediluvian types who studied Classics (Latin and Greek) at university. But having been heading that way for many years, I didn't find myself as gripped by it as some (I eventually switched to theology, studying each for two years). There was one exception: Greek tragedy. These ancient plays seemed grippingly contemporary – I especially fell in love with Euripides. Sure, the plots were outlandish, with gods and demigods prancing around and wreaking havoc on the affairs of princes and cities. But the ways these dramas probed the impact on people's lives, and even psychology, was nothing short of breathtaking. They could have been describing events in the news. This was true despite what (for modern audiences) must be the plays' strangest aspect: the masks.

Imagine some great theatre, a monumental seashell carved out of a Mediterranean mountainside. At the base of this banked semicircle is the circular stage, backed by a great wall of doors, alcoves and openings on multiple levels, from which actors playing gods might intervene in the drama. All the main action takes place on the central stage, however. The genius of these buildings is that the sightlines and acoustics are perfect, despite being open to the elements. An entire audience can see and hear everything. Because all the actors wear identical clay masks, however, the one skill they never require is facial expression. Their movements are rigidly stylized as well. Instead, they must rely *entirely* on the script and their vocal skills to move audiences to tears or laughter. But this they consistently achieve.

The purpose of these masks was to focus an audience's attention on the characters and not the actors bringing them to life. The effect, I suppose, is a bit like movie stars hidden by layers of prosthetics or digital animation. The mask also reminds the audience that this is make-believe; it is pretence; it is in fact a lie. All acting is lying. But here is the great paradox of drama: if these lies are acted convincingly, truth (whether about reality or relationships) gets conveyed powerfully.

We are perfectly familiar with this, and, in our entertainment-obsessed world, we applaud those who can pull off the widest range of parts.

But should we always be so impressed? The ancient Greek word for actor was *hypocritēs* (ὑποκρῐτής), which, at first, only implied someone who explained or interpreted something. But by New Testament times, it was more negative. It suggested someone who was untrustworthy. They pretended to be one thing while underneath being something else; they presented a good front to mask their reality.

Of course, it needs to be recognized that this is not *always* negative. Temporary masks have their place, and nearly all of us make use of them. On occasion, it may even be *right* to use them. We really shouldn't blurt out every thought that pops into our heads. That usually does more harm than good. Self-control is an important virtue, and so this type of mask is as much for others' protection as anything else.

At other times, it is neither appropriate nor necessary for those around us to be aware of every vulnerability or anxiety. A mask is thus a form of protection, necessary to shield emotional wounds from being aggravated, or from being exposed at an inappropriate moment. It is an act, in some ways – 'I'm fine,' we say – a pretence that all is well. That is not a lie as such, but an act of self-defence. As one good friend remarked to me, 'fine' can actually serve as an acronym, standing for 'Feelings Inside Not Expressed!'. It is an understandable mask, and if we never made use of it, we would probably never escape those after-church conversations that already seem interminable enough.

This mask is particularly important for those in Christian ministry. As we seek to pastor and love others, especially the vulnerable, there are times when we must swallow our pride or irritation, ignore our own needs or pressing concerns, for the sake of the urgent or important. We must show consistency and integrity, of course. But when I climb into a pulpit, I may be feeling 1,001 different things, most of which would be irrelevant, inappropriate or unhelpful to mention. We have a duty to teach what is true and healthy, even if we might wish to be miles away. We act out of Christian duty, which invariably conflicts with our emotions and passions. This is true even in normal family life, where it might be necessary to park a discussion or argument because of something more pressing (such as friends coming for a meal). Unsurprisingly, it is necessary in upfront ministry as well. This is not avoidance, but finding the right moment (unless, of course, we don't return to it).

In the strictest sense, that could be defined as hypocrisy. We *are* pretending. We *are* acting. But because of the complexity of human nature, there is a sense in which none of us can avoid being hypocritical to some degree. None of us ever has perfectly aligned motives or desires. Even Jesus found himself in great conflict in the Garden of Gethsemane – his deepest fears were militating against his determination to do his Father's will (Matthew 26:36–46).

What matters, I suppose, is how regularly this happens when doing our duty. No-one can be expected to hold in constant balance their duty and passions, their beliefs, feelings and actions, their words and deeds. Being 'out of sync' is not hypocrisy – only the pretence of always being 'in sync' is. And this is where we begin to home in on what Jesus was so critical of. He lambasted the Pharisees for their claims to perfection and their subsequent self-righteous contempt for others:

> You are like whitewashed tombs, which look beautiful on the outside but on the inside are full of the bones of the dead and everything unclean. In the same way, on the outside you appear to people as righteous but on the inside you are full of hypocrisy and wickedness.
> (Matthew 23:27–28)

The issue is how honest we are about our weakness and flaws.

Self-defence masks are like that. They are not Pharisaical, they rarely claim perfection, nor do they make people self-righteous. The problem comes when wearing them becomes a habitual, or even permanent, way of being. This was what happened to me. Since childhood, I had developed self-defence habits that kept me going temporarily, but which proved unsustainable long-term. It was as if the ancient actor's mask had become glued to my face. I played a part – of the approachable, sorted, though emotionally up and down, friend, and later pastor. So, for example, after I first mentioned my depression diagnosis in public (during a question and answer session at a church retreat), a friend came up to me in shock. She remarked that had she known there was a church staff member with this diagnosis, she would never have guessed it was me.

But this mask was artificial. It concealed reality and inhibited support. Nobody who's 'fine' needs help . . . right? So the mask inevitably started cracking, revealing that things really were not right.

As I consider how things developed in the subsequent years, three specific moments are lodged in my mind as indicative of how bad things had become.

## Three signs that could not be ignored

### Fear: tears before beauty

Just weeks after our return from four years in Kampala, Uganda, I was minding my own business in one of my favourite places in the whole world: the Wallace Collection. It's an astonishing place – a beautiful house in central London developed to showcase a remarkable private art collection. It is an oasis of beauty and calm in one of the world's most frenetic cities. Poussin, Velázquez, Titian, Gainsborough, Rubens, Canaletto . . . they're all there. If you know anything about art history, those are big names. Breathtaking!

But I always make a beeline for the Rembrandts. In particular, his portrait of his son, Titus. It is bursting with love and affection, as well as insight into this headstrong young man. What a gift for alchemy Rembrandt had – the ability to breathe life into dead strokes of paint on cloth. I could gaze for hours, lost in the moment.

And then I heard the sirens of distant police cars. I found myself transported in an altogether different way, fixed to the spot, no longer looking at the painting. Instead, I was suddenly, vividly back in Kampala, with a traffic police officer the size of a rugby prop-forward sitting in the passenger seat of my vehicle. And the tears started silently pouring.

Many of my anxieties were provoked by an inability to trust those in authority, as those who have read my book *A Wilderness of Mirrors* well know.[1] One of the darkest episodes of our Uganda years was the abduction and torture of one of my best students. We'll call him M. With his young family, M. had fled from DR Congo as a refugee, and was a gifted and experienced minister. He had already planted churches in the countries he had lived in: Rwanda and Kenya. Then, in Uganda, where he hoped finally to settle, he was offered a pastorate in one of Kampala's slum areas. In the coming months, he unearthed some illegal activity by a corrupt local politician, and so attempted to speak truth to power. As we subsequently discovered, M. was too much of a threat, and so the 'big man' arranged for him to be 'dealt with'.

One night, M. disappeared in sinister circumstances. He stepped out of the family home at around 7.30 pm wearing only his pyjamas and slippers, and then he just vanished. In great distress, M.'s wife reported the disappearance to the local police station. But it soon became apparent that the officers there were complicit, presumably paid off by the 'big man'. When we tried to follow up M.'s missing person report a day later, these files too had 'disappeared'.

A week after his disappearance, M. was dumped in a forest several hours north of Kampala, naked, drugged and horrifically injured. I can hardly bear to imagine the sight – perhaps something akin to Legion, the demon-possessed man of Mark 5. Yet, miraculously, he found help, even managing to get transport back to the capital. That evening I visited him in hospital. He was in a terrible state. And very scared.

His captors had threatened to kill him if he didn't leave Uganda. But that was easier said than done. As a vulnerable, anonymous refugee up against some evidently powerful people, nobody would risk looking after him. It was much easier for me to be involved as a foreigner. The only hope was to get him and the family out of the country legally. But, for that to happen, it had to be through the auspices of UNHCR.[2] Thus, as evidence of what this dear brother had endured, he asked me to take photographs of all his grotesque injuries. I had flashbacks for months. I dread to think of the continued impact the entire ordeal still has on M. For eighteen months or so, we were committed to keeping his family alive and safe. Generous friends in the UK and USA sent us funds to pay rent on different properties to which the family relocated every few months. It was an incredibly stressful time. We couldn't even begin to process it all until we returned to London, even though, a year before, we had experienced the ecstatic joy of receiving a text message the moment M. and his family touched down safely in Toronto.

To make matters worse for my mental state, I had twice been arrested on ridiculous charges within our first few months in Uganda by traffic police wanting bribes. I fully understood it at one level – they were expected to live on hopelessly inadequate salaries, so they would often target foreigners just before Christmas. How else could they afford gifts for their children? But the first occasion made an indelible impact on me. We had only been in the country for a few weeks, and so were borrowing a car before getting our own. Little did I know that the vehicle's tax disc on the window had expired three days before. The officer got into the passenger seat with his clipboard and wanted to see my papers. At that stage, I didn't have my Ugandan driving licence, so offered him my UK licence.

As he copied out my details, he asked with a barely suppressed smirk, 'Ah! Are you a reverend?'

'Yes, I am.'

'Well, *Caesar* has you now!'

For this green and relatively innocent Brit from a privileged and safe background, this was a shock, to say the least. I've replayed those words often. They betray a startling intelligence and insight that could only have come from more than a passing acquaintance of the New Testament world. They seemed maliciously calculated to convey maximum unease.

He then boomed, 'Buy me a crate of beer!'

'I don't think that's right, is it?'

'No, it's *wrong*,' he said and grinned.

Our stand-off continued for the best part of an hour, and then, eventually, he asked me to drop him back near his post, and I went on my way. But I was a wreck when I reached home.

The Lord clearly had a strange sense of humour. Some time later, I found myself preaching inside the national police barracks headquarters one Sunday morning. I had got to know a number of Christian officers who genuinely wanted to live differently, but their lives were almost unbearable at times. This did help me to appreciate their predicament, but it never cured my anxieties. On my daily drive to college, police checkpoints were common, with perhaps a fortnightly stop to examine papers. It meant that I sometimes needed a moment in prayer for sufficient calm just to set off to work.

Being back in London didn't seem to change anything. I was still anxious about the police. Or *any* authority or institution, for that matter. Then, in around 2005 / 2006, there was some legislation going through the British Parliament that could have made life much more difficult for Christian ministers to work – it made the possibility of arrest seem entirely plausible. Fortunately, it was soon defeated, although, as it happened, by only one vote.[3]

But when I stood rooted to the spot in the Rembrandt room, I was convinced it was the last time I'd be able to see such beauty. The sirens were coming for me. I was going down. For life. And I'd be tortured. Just like M. And I couldn't bear it. So down the tears poured. Nothing could stop them.

This was the first of several panic attacks over the coming months. It was clearly abnormal. And irrational. Something was badly wrong.

No mask could possibly conceal that now.

### Shame: silenced in the snow
Some years later, I spent a week staying with friends in Berlin. I was there during my sabbatical in 2013 to do background research for *A Wilderness of Mirrors*, and it was my first visit to that great city. Berlin's unique historical significance, particularly during the Cold War, had long been a source of great fascination for me.

On one particular day, I visited the headquarters of the Stasi (East Germany's infamous secret police) which was chilling in its nondescript functionality and minimalism.[4]

I then retraced, on foot, a section of the route of the Berlin Wall, including the now over-touristy Checkpoint Charlie. As one might expect, it was a day to stir all kinds of emotions and thoughts.

I then headed back to my hosts, but distractedly boarded the wrong tram. It was no great disaster. I simply got off at the nearest stop and waited for the next one in the opposite direction. I found myself standing at a deserted passenger shelter at dusk, in a completely unknown part of what had been East Berlin, just as snow was beginning to fall. One couldn't have contrived a better set-up for an agent rendezvous in a spy thriller. Only a few years before, my incompetence would have put me in a genuinely frightening predicament. But not in 2013. I wasn't afraid. Instead, something far stranger happened.

As I stood in the gently swirling snow, I suddenly, but inexplicably, felt overwhelmed. Inexplicable, because it actually had nothing to do with where I was or what I was doing, as I now realize. I felt overwhelmed by a sense of shame. That's different from guilt. It's much more all-encompassing and debilitating than that. It's not simply embarrassment (the fear of which is, of course, the great British disease, and the source of most British humour) – although I was mildly embarrassed about having taken the wrong tram.

No, I was ashamed of *myself*. I was ashamed of my weakness and frailty. Why hadn't I dealt with my depression (oh, how I detest the word!)? Over seven years since my formal diagnosis, why hadn't I managed just to 'snap out of it'? I was ashamed to be the kind of person that gets depressed; ashamed to be someone who couldn't be normal, or happy, or, dare I say it, reliable; ashamed of my many failings as a husband and a father, of the way my issues affected the family so adversely;

ashamed that I, a church minister, had mental health 'issues'. After all, weren't we supposed to minister to other people and *their* issues, not wallow in the sludge of our *own*?

It was a relief to be alone at that moment – there was no need to explain my silent tears. But I look back now on that strange, solitary moment with an even greater sense of relief, because it forced me to face realities about myself and depression with greater honesty. It led to wide reading about the nature of shame, and led me even to start writing about it. I have since discovered how much more common an affliction it is in Western churches, certainly more than I had ever been led to believe. Yet it is so rarely aired or discussed, to the terrible detriment of us all.

But that was to come, only after professional help and support. Back in March 2013, I was just bewildered, lacking the vocabulary to articulate what I felt. The important thing to appreciate, though, is that I didn't recognize it as shame. The only feeling it seemed to resemble was guilt. I couldn't distinguish between the two. But that didn't make sense. Nothing I had done seemed remotely able to explain the billows of despair and lostness.

### Confusion: pounding the walls

It was now late 2015, a couple of years after my sabbatical. I had taken the strange (and, to some minds, reckless) decision to leave my amazing job after nine years on the staff of All Souls, Langham Place. There were several reasons, but the most pressing was the need for work that offered greater flexibility for managing my health. I had always longed for more time to write, and there was more than enough work to keep me occupied, even part-time, with my responsibilities for developing pastoral training in Europe for Langham Partnership. It did make sense.

What I hadn't anticipated was the accumulative effect of all this sudden change. We had to move out of our wonderful church flat in central London, to a new neighbourhood in which we knew nobody. I no longer had fixed points in my week, no longer had a clear role within a community, and was no longer on a team that met regularly. The problem with our Langham team is that we're spread out all over the globe, and so are never actually all awake at the same time! To complicate matters still further, writing by its very nature is a solitary exercise, which, as one writer friend with similar battles has observed, is not exactly conducive to well-being when battling depression.

So I found myself spiralling out of control as my world seemed to shrink. It was as if so much of the scaffolding that made life liveable had been stripped back – and I had only myself to blame. I was the one who had decided to go freelance, after all. Nobody forced me into it.

But I made mistakes with others, not least in unrealistic, and even unfair, expectations of what friendship might look like. I naturally gravitated towards the few I knew who had similar battles, because they at least could understand. Nobody else did. I was desperate for connection with others, longing for companionship in what I was going through. I didn't have the words. I just had the pain unmasked, with the nerve endings too close to the surface. It was raw.

A problem was that one of my sabbatical resolutions had been to ditch the mask, or at least try to. I'd begun to recognize its symptoms. I had spent years unwittingly giving the impression that all was well, despite needing help. So it had probably come as something of a shock to colleagues hoping I would return refreshed and renewed. Instead, I undoubtedly showed less confidence or stability. I was even asked by one

well-meaning congregation member why I 'wasn't feeling
better after my sabbatical'! The irony was that I *had* taken
positive steps by ditching the mask. I just appeared worse than
before. It must have been very confusing to those around me.
And, to be fair, I didn't tell anyone that this was what I'd
resolved!

So that autumn, I found myself alone for much of the time
in our rented north London house, with the children at school
most of the day and Rachel continuing her pioneering All
Souls ministry to carers and toddlers. Meanwhile, I was
isolated, and thus isolating myself, in a spiral of negativity. I
had all this time now when I wasn't travelling for Langham,
and I was supposed to be making the most of it for writing.
That was what I'd always wanted, wasn't it? But I couldn't
even do that. I just sat at my desk, either staring into the
middle distance or idly surfing through inane YouTube clips.
It felt pathetic . . . and selfish (generous friends were now
funding our new life).

But this perfect storm left me feeling bereft of *every single
one* of my moorings. Even the few friends I had hoped might
be sympathetic or understanding seemed too preoccupied
or fearful. I don't blame them at all – none of us really anticipated this. But I found it bewildering and terrifying.

Because the worst thing of all was the total absence
of God.

One moment sums it up. I was alone in the house, early
one evening. For whatever reason, I decided to have a shower.
Sudden waves of sorrow, fear and even anger overwhelmed
me. They began without the slightest warning. This time I
wasn't just weeping, but convulsed by tears, crying out. To
family. To friends. To God. Of course, nobody could hear me.
And nor, it seemed, could God. I was pounding the bathroom
walls with my fists and crying out for God to do something.

Anything. And then I just slumped in the shower, exhausted and depleted. It had been a rare moment of intense energy amidst hours and days of the cruel tedium of what Winston Churchill had called his 'black dog'.

It is bizarre perhaps that I never cried 'why me?'. Many do, of course, and I certainly don't blame them for that. Yet it's never been a question I have struggled with. Perhaps it is because there are just too many inexplicable horrors in this world; perhaps it is because of what we had witnessed in Africa; perhaps it is because I well appreciate how genuinely privileged my life has been. I could equally ask the same question for my many blessings.

The question that I cannot get out of my head, however, is simpler. Just 'why?' So much of mental illness, with its associated disorientating perspectives, paranoias and pains, makes no sense. It is irrational and without obvious cause. But its effects are obvious enough, if only to the sufferer. Then, there is the salt that gets poured on open wounds. Why do others seem to get it wrong so often? Why does mental illness fill some with such fear or stigma? Why does it bring out the worst do-gooding or meddling instincts in others? Why do so many with mental illness end up so alone and isolated? Why? I pounded the shower walls with that question over and over until I was spent.

Some answers can be found, of course. But they only go so far, until we come up against the limits of human understanding and divine revelation.

But, at the darkest moments, the *sole* reason why I felt I could still do business with God in my bewilderment was what he allowed to be included in the Bible. To be more precise, it was the Psalms. A God who could handle a psalmist praying these things was one that I had no right altogether to dismiss:

My tears have been my food day and night,
while people say to me all day long,
    'Where is your God?'
(Psalm 42:3)

Out of the depths I cry to you, LORD;
    Lord, hear my voice.
Let your ears be attentive
    to my cry for mercy.
(Psalm 130:1–2)

And most extraordinary of all:

    . . . your terrors have destroyed me.
All day long they surround me like a flood;
    they have completely engulfed me.
You have taken from me friend and neighbour –
    darkness is my closest friend.
(Psalm 88:16–18)

That is why I am still here, feeble sometimes, flawed always,
clinging on to the Jesus of Gethsemane and Golgotha.

PART 1:
DEEPER INTO THE DARKNESS

## 2. THE VOLCANO

I desperately needed people living in the real world, in the same world as me. A world where there might not be obvious causes, just palpable effects, where prayers don't ever seem to be heard, where days bring apparent deterioration, not improvement.

Above all, I needed friends, not fixers. And not just amongst the people around me.

In recent years, there has been a marked increase in people's openness about mental health challenges. This must be good, since it is such a common reality for so many (although I am sceptical about the statistics of quite how prevalent it is). Furthermore, talking about these challenges, with friends who understand, has profound therapeutic benefits.

This has come about, in part, because of the emergence of confessional TV and the misery memoir. There is now a proliferation of writing about, and testimonies of, the mysteries of mental pain. There seems no shortage of reading material when it comes to depression.

My problem was that hardly any helped. Or at least, it made little or no impact on what I was going through. Perhaps this is because the range of people's experience is too broad. Generalized observations or comments simply felt too far removed from me. I've read various Christian books too, but (to generalize!) these tend only to irritate. I am being unfair, I realize, but they are often too simplistic, too glib or too prescriptive, and sometimes all three. They seem to betray the fear that the slightest hint of mystery or doubt might somehow undermine God and his gospel (which is absurd). At their bleakest, they are Job's comforters in print form, who, in the guise of pastoral concern, made matters worse; as if the identification of an obvious cause would lead to a speedy improvement or answered prayer or anticipated effect.

## The words of a friend in the darkness

Thankfully, I did find at least one such friend. He's been dead for a number of years now, and I barely even registered his passing at the time. Because we only really 'met' when I read his remarkable 1990 memoir, *Darkness Visible*.[1] I'm eternally grateful to my old friend Frankie who put me onto it.

William Styron was a successful and respected man of letters, an American novelist who had made his name with *The Confessions of Nat Turner* and *Sophie's Choice*. He was at the pinnacle of his career and worldly esteem, in Paris to receive a prestigious literary prize. But on that very night, his world appeared to collapse as he walked the rain-drenched French streets. Despite never having previously had mental health problems, his equilibrium dissolved. Over the subsequent weeks, his health declined so markedly that he found himself seriously planning how to take his own life. The shock of that prompted him to check himself into hospital the next day.

All this would have remained private had Styron not been appalled by reactions to the apparent suicide in 1987 of the great Primo Levi (coincidentally, another of my literary heroes). Levi was an Italian chemist who wrote very powerfully about surviving Auschwitz.[2] In later life, though, he suffered from depression, and while some friends and writers suggest otherwise, the coroner (as well as three biographers) ruled his death as suicide. Elie Wiesel, that other holocaust survivor and literary great, remarked poignantly, 'Primo Levi died at Auschwitz forty years later.'[3]

Styron was concerned to explain, from his own experience, why someone might be driven to suicide, and therefore be entirely deserving of sympathy and understanding, not stigma or condemnation. What started life as articles in the *New York Times* and then *Vanity Fair* ended as the all-too-brief book: *Darkness Visible*, subtitled *A Memoir of Madness*.

This book is credited with being a game-changer – leading to the increased openness I mentioned at the start of this chapter.[4] More than that, it is a lifesaver. At *last*, I had found a friend in print. He clearly loved words. But, more importantly, he clearly struggled to find them.

I would never claim anything remotely close to Styron's genius. But for someone who has similarly loved words, one of the most destabilizing effects of my depression was my complete inability to describe it. This wasn't simply an intellectual problem, still less an aesthetic puzzle. It impacted on my relationships with those closest to me, especially Rachel. I could never convey what was wrong. Nothing I said, nor the suggestions they made, came close to doing it justice, and so it invariably seemed less serious than it felt. In fact, the very act of putting it into words appeared to make it much more manageable – as if giving an ailment a name somehow revealed the automatic door to a potential 'cure'.

It somehow made it all too easy. So, much to Rachel's loving but agonized frustration, this psychological dyslexia rendered me mute.

Styron recognized this:

> Depression is a disorder of mood, so mysteriously painful and elusive in the way it becomes known to the self – to the mediating intellect – as to verge close to being beyond description. It thus remains nearly incomprehensible to those who have not experienced it in its extreme mode, although the gloom, 'the blues' which people go through occasionally and associate with the general hassle of everyday existence are of such prevalence that they do give many individuals a hint of the illness in its catastrophic form.[5]

He goes on:

> That the word 'indescribable' should present itself is not fortuitous, since it has to be emphasized that if the pain were readily describable most of the countless sufferers from this ancient affliction would have been able to confidently depict for their friends and loved ones (even their physicians) some of the actual dimensions of their torment, and perhaps elicit a comprehension that has been generally lacking . . .[6]

But then, with wonderful skill and art, Styron proceeds to do just that, describing the indescribable, as only great writers can. That is why we need them. Of course, he could never do it perfectly. But he didn't need to. Not for me, anyway. He simply placed my feet on the right track, a path up the rock face I hadn't actually believed existed, by conveying his own experiences. He gave me my first verbal footholds. I didn't know exactly where this path would lead; I didn't know what I could realistically hope for. But he enabled me to start walking.

In the end, that was of far greater value than published psychological analyses, self-help books or even Christian pastorals. By limiting his scope to his own life, without attempting generalization or prescription, he ended up, paradoxically, writing a book that has the broadest resonance.

## The only words that will do

I quickly gained a crucial insight from my new friendship. Styron recognized how dependent the path through darkness often is on metaphors. This explains why poems and songs can be so helpful to sufferers. His book's title is a case in point, taken from Milton's evocation of hell's darkness, that ultimate indescribable place:

> No light, but rather darkness visible
> Serv'd onely to discover sights of woe,
> Regions of sorrow, doleful shades, where peace
> And rest can never dwell, hope never comes
> That comes to all; but torture without end
> Still urges, and a fiery Deluge, fed
> With ever-burning Sulphur unconsum'd.
> (*Paradise Lost*, I. 63–69)

Milton presumably did not intend to describe mental illness here. But these lines are surprisingly apposite. Or, at least, they evoke something of the pain when in the midst of it. Which is the best we can hope for.

So the word 'depression' is a non-starter. I detest it. So does Styron, I think.

It comes nowhere close to describing the reality, and it has become far too commonplace – used of the aftermath of a mild setback, or a week of overwork, or a head cold that won't shift. None of these is especially fun – and they deserve sympathy, no doubt. And they might make someone feel low. But feeling low, quite emphatically, is not depression. It can usually be dealt with by a hot bath, an early night or a walk with the dog. As a metaphor, depression is hopeless.

So Styron hunts down an alternative:

> As one who has suffered from the malady *in extremis* yet returned to tell the tale, I would lobby for a truly arresting designation. 'Brainstorm,' for instance, has unfortunately been pre-empted to describe, somewhat jocularly, intellectual inspiration. But something along these lines is needed. Told that someone's mood disorder has evolved into a storm – a veritable howling tempest in the brain, which is indeed what a clinical depression resembles like nothing else – even the uninformed layman might display sympathy rather than the standard reaction that 'depression' evokes, something akin to 'So what?' or 'You'll pull out of it' or 'We all have bad days.' The phrase 'nervous breakdown' seems to be on its way out, certainly deservedly so, owing to its insinuation of vague spinelessness, but we still seem destined to be saddled with 'depression' until a better, sturdier name is created.[7]

I quite like 'brainstorm'. It does fit. Above all, it captures the intensity and activity of the experience. Or, to put it another way, it prevents anyone presuming that it is all just passivity. It might lead to external passivity – a common symptom is the inability to get out of bed in the morning. But that should not imply internal passivity. Unfortunately.

In my own case, though, brainstorm doesn't quite nail it. So, I have started using 'brain blizzard'. Now, the UK does not really get 'proper weather', so, despite the frequent claims of British forecasters, we barely know the meaning of heatwaves, storms and blizzards. American friends just laugh at how quaint and mild our weather threats usually are. So I have never experienced a 'whiteout' first-hand, the moment when the horizon disappears in a snowstorm, leaving someone without any reference points at all. It is violent, the result of huge, unseen, natural forces at work, and it leaves a person completely disorientated.

Now, *that* is more like it. A violent disorientation.

But there is another feature which needs inclusion, one that we still haven't quite grasped. It is still elemental, it is still violent, but for some of the time, it remains invisible. 'Dormant' might be a better term. So I sometimes resort to adding something more geological to the meteorological.

### Tectonic plates and swirling lava

It hit me during a BBC nature programme, no doubt narrated by David Attenborough. I can't recall much, apart from the footage of bubbling, lethal, viscous lava seeping out of the earth's crust. It seeps out inexorably, gorging itself on every-thing in its path. It is astonishing to consider that the entire planet's crust constrains lava like this. Yet it only emerges into the open, sometimes with inconceivable violence, at specific spots around the world.

Over twenty years ago, I had a friend who was trying to complete a PhD in volcanology. He worked on it for years, but was driven by a profound sense of social responsibility. I forget the details, and we have long lost touch, but he was convinced he had discovered a way to improve the prediction time for a volcanic eruption. If right, countless lives could be saved. There are many indicators, both long-term and short-term, which suggest that an eruption is imminent. Thus, in 2000, scientists predicted that Popocatépetl, the volcano outside Mexico City, was about to erupt, perhaps within the next two days. The government initiated a huge-scale evacuation. Sure enough, two days later it had its largest eruption for a millennium. Without a single loss of life.

But it is almost impossible to be much more specific. My friend thought that he had found a way. Unfortunately, his method literally added only a few seconds to the average countdown. He was devastated, and ended up giving up his research. We can only hope that matters have developed in the field since then.

Depression has felt volcanic at times. It may lie relatively dormant for some time, while its lava and force are constantly shielded beneath the tectonic plates. Without warning, it then forces its way through, plunging the mind into a riot of irrational thoughts that discombobulate and terrify. And I just don't see it coming. There may not be a specific catalyst or trigger at all. Or perhaps, to be more accurate, there may be no *apparent* catalyst, even after I wrack my brains to retrace my mental steps. The power of human memory is astonishing – smells, sounds, songs or circumstances can evoke a past moment, which in turn can provoke a long-forgotten feeling, especially if it has a downward trajectory.

Strangely enough, people nearby may not notice much outward change, especially if the mask is still intact. I'll come to that. But I'll be caught out by an eruption of psychological pain. It feels like sudden grief and despair without an immediately obvious loss. Or it might manifest as uncontrollable anxiety and dread. There might have been occasional hints that this was coming, but nothing to prepare one for the eruption. Of course, if there *are* external factors and triggers, then it is all the worse for that. But even if there is an escape route from these, there is no escaping one's own mind. Just the potential of that dormant havoc is scary enough.

Stranger still is this psychological volcano's physical effects. This aspect certainly caught me by surprise. Here's Styron again:

> What I had begun to discover is that, mysteriously and in ways that are totally remote from normal experience, the gray drizzle of horror induced by depression takes on the quality of physical pain. But it is not an immediately identifiable pain, like that of a broken limb. It may be more accurate to say that despair, owing to some evil trick played upon the sick brain by the inhabiting psyche, comes to resemble the diabolical discomfort of being imprisoned in a fiercely overheated room. And because no breeze stirs this cauldron, because there is no escape from this smothering confinement, it is entirely natural that the victim begins to think ceaselessly of oblivion.[8]

This will naturally affect each person differently, but I have experienced a range of these symptoms at various points.

### Racing adrenaline and a pumping heart

This is the typical experience of someone battling depression's close relative, anxiety. I have had this for hours at a time. Sometimes, I wake up with it. As my eyes open, my first conscious thought is to be aware of a dull, settled, but implacable, dread in the pit of my stomach. It's a bit like the aftermath of experiencing a shock when your limbs suddenly feel feeble and insubstantial (as you might if someone yanks you away from the kerb just before you step in front of a lorry). But it never seems to die down. At one point, I was prescribed anxiety medication which actually had the opposite effect, *intensifying*, rather than alleviating, the sensation! I came off this quickly, but it took a few weeks for my system to have its residue washed out. Even without that, though, relaxation is impossible and exhaustion inevitable.

## Apparent passivity

To the outside world, this tectonic activity may simply resemble agitation or nervousness. Or perhaps it is sitting completely still, staring out of the window. But this apparent calm, or even sullenness, conceals an inner chaos, with every last sinew dedicated to keeping one's head above water. Perhaps it's rather like an exhausted shipwreck perpetually treading water in the open seas. The (irrational?) terror concerns what will happen when we no longer have the energy. Will we go under? Will we drown? Or, to return to the volcano briefly, every effort is focused on keeping the tectonic plates in place. Because if the eruption breaks out into the outside world, what will happen then?

I'm all too aware of mixing and manipulating my metaphors here. But that's precisely the point. None of them alone does it justice.

## Lifting weights

Some experience this expenditure of energy as resembling reaching the end of a rigorous gym workout (an activity I have always done my best to avoid, if I can possibly help it). Muscles quiver and ache, with the whole body feeling feeble, as if it has been turned to jelly. This is why they experience depression as a very literal heaviness, as if living on a planet with double earth's gravity. Just going to the shops can feel as debilitating as assaulting Mount Everest.[9] No wonder some find it hard to get out of bed in the morning. This is not simply a matter of feeling low – it's far worse than that.

For some reason, I've never been keen on long lie-ins. I might stay in bed to read a book for a bit, but just lying in bed all day has never appealed. But this does not mean I am productive when I do get up. There have been times when, if I lived alone, I could easily have sat in a darkened room all day without doing a single thing. (It is hard to do that while living in a house with two teenagers!) Gravity seems to make life heavier and the air too thick to breathe. This isn't agoraphobia, or anything like that. It's not anxiety about other people. It's more the effort of existence. That takes everything you've got.

### Jitters and irritants

Sudden noises or surprises can be tricky. Since getting a real dog (which, as it happens, is black, and for partly therapeutic reasons), this mainly happens now when she suddenly barks at the postman! But I seem to jump right out of my skin, and it can take me considerable time to regain an equilibrium.

It is an overreaction, of course. But that doesn't make it any easier.

### Sleepless nights

Insomnia is a classic feature of depression. It is incongruous, though, because one would think that the exhaustion of all this psychological effort would lead to going out like a light.

But despite attempting what the experts call good 'sleep hygiene' (which includes, for example, being careful what you do in the couple of hours before bedtime), I seem to get into stupid patterns of wakefulness. When we lived in our flat, it was fine – the concrete floors meant that I could slip out to the sitting room to read without bothering anyone else. But now we are in a house of creaking floorboards and stairs, that is harder to do. So sometimes I just lie awake, changing positions every now and then to get more comfortable, trying to keep my mind from drifting into unhelpful thought patterns. The hardest thing is to stifle the panic from knowing one *ought* to sleep. Needless to say, the net result is deeper tiredness.

## When ancient words are a relief

Reading Styron had an unexpected consequence, one that now feels so frustrating, so stupid! As he opened my eyes to the therapeutic importance of metaphors, I suddenly appreciated what had been right in front of my nose all along. I had taught about them many times, sometimes in careful and unhurried explanations from the pulpit. I knew it, but I didn't *know* it. This was the way that the Bible constantly uses metaphor to point to the indescribable – after all, it is impossible to do justice to God's true nature and character in mere human words, as Isaiah knew:

> As the heavens are higher than the earth,
>    so are my ways higher than your ways
>    and my thoughts than your thoughts.
> (Isaiah 55:9)

This is *not* to suggest there are *no words* at all; merely that we are ultimately dependent on God's revelation of his nature, using words that are aggravatingly limited by the narrowness of human experience.

But it is not just God we struggle to find words for. It is the life of discipleship in a broken world. Some things do not make sense. Pain and suffering bewilder and confuse. Evil destroys good things; it never creates or improves. It is irrational. It is, therefore, also beyond words.

This is surely why the Psalms burst with metaphors, and why they have been so treasured.

King David wasn't the only poet to have work included in the Jewish Scriptures, of course, but he wrote a large proportion of the Psalms. He had lived what might euphemistically be termed a 'varied' life – great highs and achievements, interspersed with the darkest of valleys and fears, as well as behaviour that could be ruthless, arrogant and selfish. But even he could never have literally experienced all the hardships he sings about. He used metaphors.

The Psalms had always been important to me. But now, as the result of a secular novelist's genius, they became my oxygen tanks. Or even my stethoscope. They used images that, I now fully appreciate, *did* correspond to what was going on in my head. I just never made the connection somehow. The psalmist gave words to the internal turmoil that I could now hear with more clarity.

This is not the place for a full survey, but even a cursory glance through the first pages of the book of Psalms reveals a remarkable diversity (see the first table). All but three (10, 42, 46) come from David's pen. Sometimes they describe the pain of his predicament; at other times, they plead for rescue. But *all* of them show a remarkable ability to capture with uncanny precision what it *feels* like.

Those last verses, from Psalm 55, have helped me put the unspeakable into pleading words on more than a few occasions. What balm it is to find my own experience echoed in a king's three-millennia-old prayer! It was also encouraging in a way to find the psalmist reaching for geological and meteorological metaphors.

Of course, the Psalms never leave us there.

They are poetic testimonies of confidence in God's goodness, even in the midst of these dark times. They are always

| **Feeling under threat (by enemies real or imagined)** | |
|---|---|
| 7:2 | They will tear me apart like a lion<br>        and rip me to pieces with no one to rescue me. |
| 14:4 | They devour my people as though eating bread. |
| 17:8–9 | Keep me as the apple of your eye;<br>        hide me in the shadow of your wings<br>from the wicked who are out to destroy me,<br>        from my mortal enemies who surround me. |
| 22:6–7 | But I am a worm and not a man,<br>        scorned by everyone, despised by the people.<br>All who see me mock me;<br>        they hurl insults, shaking their heads. |
| 31:11–12 | Because of all my enemies,<br>        I am the utter contempt of my neighbours<br>and an object of dread to my closest friends –<br>        those who see me on the street flee from me.<br>I am forgotten as though I were dead;<br>        I have become like broken pottery. |
| **Overwhelmed by pain, isolation and fear** | |
| 10:1 | Why, Lord, do you stand far off?<br>        Why do you hide yourself in times of trouble? |
| 13:1–2 | How long, Lord? Will you forget me for ever?<br>        How long will you hide your face from me?<br>How long must I wrestle with my thoughts<br>        and day after day have sorrow in my heart?<br>        How long will my enemy triumph over me? |
| 38:5–8 | My wounds fester and are loathsome<br>        because of my sinful folly.<br>I am bowed down and brought very low;<br>        all day long I go about mourning.<br>My back is filled with searing pain;<br>        there is no health in my body.<br>I am feeble and utterly crushed;<br>        I groan in anguish of heart. |

| 42:1–3 | As the deer pants for streams of water,<br>    so my soul pants for you, my God.<br>My soul thirsts for God, for the living God.<br>    When can I go and meet with God?<br>My tears have been my food day and night,<br>    while people say to me all day long,<br>      'Where is your God?' |
|---|---|
| **Sinking into despair** | |
| 22:14–15 | I am poured out like water,<br>    and all my bones are out of joint.<br>My heart has turned to wax;<br>    it has melted within me.<br>My mouth is dried up like a potsherd,<br>    and my tongue sticks to the roof of my mouth;<br>    you lay me in the dust of death. |
| 42:7 | Deep calls to deep<br>    in the roar of your waterfalls;<br>all your waves and breakers<br>    have swept over me. |
| 55:4–8 | My heart is in anguish within me;<br>    the terrors of death have fallen on me.<br>Fear and trembling have beset me;<br>    horror has overwhelmed me.<br>I said, 'Oh, that I had the wings of a dove!<br>    I would fly away and be at rest.<br>I would flee far away<br>    and stay in the desert;<br>I would hurry to my place of shelter,<br>    far from the tempest and storm.' |

songs of faith. This explains why even the darkest psalms find glimmers of hope in the dark (see the second table).

But this is never an unthinking, unfeeling or unrealistic faith. It is always rooted in genuine experience and perception. The Psalms would never have passed the tests of time if they

| God in the midst of the pain | |
|---|---|
| 7:10 | My shield is God Most High. |
| 9:9 | The LORD is a refuge for the oppressed,<br>    a stronghold in times of trouble. |
| 18:2 | The LORD is my rock, my fortress and my deliverer;<br>    my God is my rock, in whom I take refuge,<br>    my shield and the horn of my salvation, my<br>        stronghold. |
| 40:1–2 | I waited patiently for the LORD;<br>    he turned to me and heard my cry.<br>He lifted me out of the slimy pit,<br>    out of the mud and mire;<br>he set my feet on a rock<br>    and gave me a firm place to stand. |
| 46:1–3 | God is our refuge and strength,<br>    an ever-present help in trouble.<br>Therefore we will not fear, though the earth give way<br>    and the mountains fall into the heart of the sea,<br>though its waters roar and foam<br>    and the mountains quake with their surging. |

weren't. This inevitably means that these ancient verses can be quite difficult, especially for those who prefer life, the universe and God to conform to nice and predictable frameworks. But life has a constant habit of disrupting our frameworks. And our sense of God.

This explains why the psalmist can be quite so daring. On occasion, he might actually *blame* God. After all, if he is sovereign, he must ultimately be responsible for his suffering. That is perhaps the greatest mystery of life in a broken world. But while evil deeds may indeed bring about suffering (such as in Psalm 38 here), there *is* such a thing as innocent suffering – suffering that results from doing the right thing, and suffering that has no reasons or makes no sense. This is a much more common Bible theme than the modern counter-parts of Job's comforters acknowledge. So, while the psalmist struggles or pleads for help, he never denies the mystery.

This is what makes Psalm 88 one of the most extraordinary chapters in the Bible. It starts with urgent prayer, like many other psalms:

> You have put me in the lowest pit,
>> in the darkest depths.
> Your wrath lies heavily on me;
>> you have overwhelmed me with all your waves.
> You have taken from me my closest friends
>> and have made me repulsive to them.
> I am confined and cannot escape;
>> my eyes are dim with grief.
> (Psalm 88:6–9)

His despair overwhelms him, especially because he senses that it comes as the result of divine punishment. But to make matters worse, he perseveres in having his morning devotional times with God, but hears *nothing* from him. Is he there? Can he hear? Will he intervene? Does he even care? The writer, one Heman the Ezrahite, draws the only conclusion apparently available. The answer to each question is 'No' because nothing has changed. He is still in agony.

So look how it ends:

> But I cry to you for help, LORD;
>> in the morning my prayer comes before you.
> Why, LORD, do you reject me
>> and hide your face from me?
> From my youth I have suffered and been close to death;
>> I have borne your terrors and am in despair.

Your wrath has swept over me;
    your terrors have destroyed me.
All day long they surround me like a flood;
    they have completely engulfed me.
You have taken from me friend and neighbour –
    darkness is my closest friend.
(Psalm 88:13–18)

I had never taken that psalm in before. I am sure I must have read it at some point – and probably sung it (over the years since childhood, I had sung in several choirs that followed the English cathedral tradition of psalm chanting). But I had never appreciated the revolution it represents.

The paradoxes tumble out, once you set your mind to it:

- The Bible is held to be the revelation of God to us. He is speaking to us. It can never be reduced simply to an expression of human groping in the dark after God (as many critical theologians have claimed).
- But the Bible does contain the Psalms – which are, by their very nature, a human expression of seeking and praying to God.
- Yet, ever since the Psalms were first prayed, God seems to have spoken to his people through these ancient prayers to him. Occasionally, he actually uses the experience of David (who as king was the greatest messiah in Israel's history) to prefigure and thus prophesy about the experiences of the greatest Messiah of all. This is clearest in Psalm 22.
- But even in the psalms that are not explicitly predictive, God speaks through them at the level of giving us words for the times when we lack them. They effectively say, it is OK to say these things to me.

Psalm 88's closing words blew me away. Here is no hope; there seems no faith. It is almost blasphemous – God is meant to be so good that he is our utterly reliable friend. But to claim that 'darkness is my closest friend' is to appear to reject God. At the very least, it illustrates a lost confidence in him.

But the fact remains that this verse is in the Bible. There it has sat for nearly 3,000 years!

So God must be saying it is OK to say this – if you feel like it. This does not mean that the words are accurate. The psalmist would never let us get away with that. But they are real words. So here is the final paradox. Heman the Ezrahite expresses *in prayer to God* what it feels like to have no God at all. He prays in despair and because of his despair. Even though that seems like the last thing one should do if there is no God at work. So, to my mind, Psalm 88 is unexpectedly one of the Bible's most liberating chapters.

To understand why, we need to think a little more about the significance of 'darkness is my closest friend'. This brings me to the metaphor to which I have resorted more than any other: the cave.

## 3. THE CAVE

I sometimes wish I was battling a more tangible or obvious condition. I've never been unusually resilient when it comes to physical pain, but I guess I have inherited at least some of the previous generation's stoicism. Keep on keeping on, don't complain, just get on with making the best of a bad job. That's the spirit! At least a more straightforwardly diagnosed complaint would make some sense. There would be a much clearer target to aim for.

Problems in the mind exist on a different plane altogether. Of course, such is the power of the brain that mental disturbances can have profound physical effects, as we have seen. But mental illness, by definition, makes little sense. It corrodes our equilibrium, our perceptions of reality. This fact alone should immediately sound an implicit warning to those who prefer their problems neatly packaged and swiftly cured. Not even mental health professionals (who spend whole lifetimes working at it) manage that. It will never simply be a matter of chancing upon the right word, or offering a nice day out, or giving a big hug. All I can say is, if that's your approach, please stay away! Keep your glib Bible quotes and cheesy platitudes to yourself.

But this touches on one of the toughest aspects. Coping with others, full stop. Depressive illness generates a gnawing fear that can make one cower at the sound of approaching footsteps. It is a curse that makes one withdraw in self-defence. Its endgame is solitary confinement, deceiving us into the thought that we are better off alone. That is, of course, nonsense. We desperately need other people . . . especially amid the darkness. We may also long for it. But what we crave, we dread. We are thus ensnared in the hell of depression's cave.

## Chained in the cave

The great John Bunyan was himself chained up. Literally. His crime was preaching the Christian message without a Church of England licence – a practice declared illegal after the restoration of England's monarchy in 1660. He knew first-hand what imprisonment meant. Yet it was during his incarceration that he began his masterpiece, *The Pilgrim's Progress*. This narrates the allegorical journey of Christian, the pilgrim whose conversion prompts him to travel from his home in the City of Destruction to the Celestial City.

One of Christian's most striking encounters is with Giant Despair. At this point, he is accompanied by Hopeful, but they get lost, just as a vicious, nocturnal thunderstorm begins. The deluge makes them feel as if they 'have been drowned nine or ten times'. Despite this, they have no option in the darkness but to try to sleep in the open fields. It is no surprise, then, that this grim night has repercussions, which Bunyan's ingenious imagination vividly captures.

The pilgrims discover in the morning that their sleeping spot has a terrifying owner. Giant Despair captures them for trespassing and flings them into his 'very dark dungeon, nasty and stinking to the spirits of these two men'. There they suffer for four days, starved of food, light and company. Notice how Bunyan describes their predicament. They were without 'any to ask how they did; they . . . were far from friends and acquaintances'. This then culminates in a brutal beating that leaves them almost senseless. Then, on the advice of his wife, Giant Despair decides to save himself the bother of killing them by trying to persuade them to take their own lives.[1] It is a terrible scene.

Bunyan habitually littered his narrative with Scripture references, to help readers discover the biblical inspiration for his imagination. So which verse would best fit here? Sure enough, he points the reader to the last verse of Psalm 88. Christian and Hopeful experience the agony of darkness being their 'closest friend'.

This is an uncannily accurate evocation of depression. Bunyan was clearly all too familiar with its pain. He knew its darkness, its chains, its isolation. He knew how closely related it can be to physical ailments like exhaustion and hunger. But he also connected it to the lostness that is so often a precursor to despair.

We will return to Bunyan's account at a later stage, but, for now, we only need note the intensity of the dungeon experience. No wonder Bunyan's scene has resonated with countless readers down the centuries.

Despite that, the prison cell imagery doesn't quite nail it for me. Perhaps it is because it is man-made, and therefore somehow too concrete or symmetrical. I cannot say for sure. Instead, I prefer the cave metaphor, even though its effects are almost identical. In the youth camps which I used to help with while at university, one of the most popular activities was caving. I braved it only once. That was easily enough.

There were places where the only way forward was to crawl on one's stomach through gaps that left only a centimetre or two of space above one's head. What on earth is the fun in that?

Caves are more mysterious, dank and intimidating in their organic gloom. They seem to extend endlessly into some vast labyrinth. No wonder they are a setting for nightmares and horror stories. But there's a deeper reason for the usefulness of the imagery. Caves can function as vast echo chambers. Once trapped inside, the only voice we can hear clearly is our own.

We might pray, calling out to God for connections when no-one else seems to hear. But so often it feels futile.

But then, remarkably, King David felt the same:

How long, LORD? Will you forget me for ever?
    How long will you hide your face from me?
How long must I wrestle with my thoughts
    and day after day have sorrow in my heart?
    How long will my enemy triumph over me?
(Psalm 13:1–2)

## Deafened in the cave

So there we sit, in the bleak gloom of the depression cave, isolated and fearful. We rerun recent conversations, or even snippets of long-past conversations. Repeatedly. As if on a loop. Our memories are rarely reliable at the best of times, but the nature of depression is that it functions as a distortion filter. With great effectiveness, it weeds out any encouragements or positivity. So effective is it, in fact, that it even seems to have a malice all its own. I suspect this is one reason why Winston Churchill called his own bouts of depression the 'black dog'. It feels at times like an outside force, a parasitical invader that saps energy and crushes spirits.

Of course, it isn't literally like that – but the notion of the black dog has captured many since Churchill, particularly through the excellent graphic books by Australian artist Matthew Johnstone.[2] The hound is on the prowl and is aggressively selfish. It deludes us into thinking it is all-sufficient, that we don't need others because they will only hurt us even more.

So the negative words ricochet off the cave walls, as we sit paralysed, trying to make sense of it all.

- Fred was right, you know. He nailed it – you really shouldn't be doing that job. It's way beyond you. Just who do you think you are?
- I completely lost it with the kids last night. What a disaster. They're never going to forget it, let alone forgive me. They'll need therapy for years. What a loser of a father.
- I totally get why Emily reacted. I'm always getting it wrong. She's so much better off without me around.
- They were bored to tears during Sunday's sermon. Man, it's just so humiliating. So public. What a loser.
- If only they knew what I was really like. Thank goodness they can't see inside. But God can. Oh God, I can't take this any more. You're better off without me.
- You must be so disappointed in me, Lord. No. Correction. You ARE so disappointed in me. FACT. And there's never any going back from disappointment, is there? I'm basically stuffed.

And so on it goes. The dog thrives on it all, like a dung beetle, while we wilt under the weight of failure and gloom, in some kind of psychological zero-sum game.

One of my spiritual heroes is the poet William Cowper (1731–1800). He was a contemporary of some of Britain's greatest Christian leaders, William Wilberforce and the Clapham Sect. In fact, he sometimes functioned as the group's unofficial poet laureate. But one of his most loyal friends was his neighbour in Olney, that repentant slave trader, hymn writer and pastor, John Newton. Newton encouraged him in his writing, and sustained him in his darkest hours. If it hadn't been for his small group of friends, Cowper would have sunk even lower. As it was, he did attempt suicide, and was removed to an asylum more than once. The conditions in those infernal places hardly bear thinking about.

Cowper found the internal ricochets unbearable. So, at one point, he wrote this in his journal,

> I laid myself down in bed, howling with horror, while
> my knees smote against each other. In this condition
> my brother found me; the first word I spoke to him (and
> I remember the very expression) was, 'Oh brother, I am
> damned – damned. Think of eternity, and then think what
> it is to be damned.'[3]

A year before his death, he wrote *The Castaway*, in which he imagines being one of two men going overboard at sea, taking it as a picture of being condemned for his sins:

> No voice divine the storm allay'd,
> No light propitious shone;
> When, snatch'd from all effectual aid,
> We perish'd, each alone:
> But I beneath a rougher sea,
> And whelm'd in deeper gulfs than he.

It's a vicious circle. I can't risk getting too close to others, because they will discover what I'm really like. Then they will say the kinds of things I've heard all too often. Which will crush me even more. So I stay away. But by staying away, I have no means of countering the negativity echoing in my head, no means of making the connections with others that I so crave. I simply don't believe that they have anything different to say.

This is how the dog likes it. It keeps us exactly where it can control us. Thus, the chains binding us to the cave of isolation seem unbreakable. It's absurd. But it's reality.

However, there is another way that the dog isolates the depressed person in the cave.


**Alone in the cave**

This is subtly different from depression's isolating effect just mentioned, although it is perhaps a contributory factor. This is the loneliness that results from the affliction being one that others cannot possibly comprehend or relate to.

As I have already said, we need words to communicate what is going on inside our heads. So, when adequate words can't be found, it is so frustrating. But this leads to a catch-22 situation. Because we are unable to find the words, our friends and loved ones cannot begin to grasp the problem. They may not recognize its seriousness, which is of course entirely understandable. They are therefore unable to support in the most appropriate way. This leads to frustration for the one depressed, and feelings of inadequacy for the ones who care.

But it goes beyond a lack of words. The person who has thankfully managed to avoid mental illness will never really be able to relate to the pain of it. They might sympathize –

they certainly ought to – but they will rarely be able to empathize. The experience is just too alien and inaccessible.

This shows itself in saying the wrong things – too glib or pat, or being frozen into saying nothing out of fear of saying the wrong thing. That might come across as insensitivity or lack of awareness. Even well-meant words might make matters worse. At best, they fail to connect with the pain, and thus the sense of isolation is ratcheted up. It's as if the cave has made the words from those who haven't experienced mental illness sound muffled. You can tell that someone 'out there' is uttering words, perhaps – but they sound incoherent, meaningless even. They certainly do not connect or help. Sometimes, you even end up having to console the comforter for their frustrated failure to be comforting!

This is why it makes such a difference to meet someone else in a similar situation. What relief it is to meet a friend in the cave!

**Friends in the cave?**

A while back, we had a newly married couple for a meal at our flat. They had been friends for several years, and so we had some insight into their backgrounds. But this time, they had come specifically to talk through some of the difficult things in their past, particularly from the wife's childhood. She was doing amazingly well, despite these challenges, but the future *felt* bleak. It was while we were having some of Rachel's legendary banoffee pie that I said something along the lines of, 'Well, of course, I have been taking anti-depressant medication for the last seven years.'

It was a very funny moment: our friend was suddenly frozen in shock, her mouth temporarily wide open and spoon immobilized in mid-air. From that point, the conversation's tone changed completely, and we could now talk, not as minister with church members, but as friends who have found each other in the cave.

Some years ago, a British newspaper invited readers to submit their best definitions of friendship and friends. Thousands of suggestions flooded in. Some of the best included:

- One who multiplies our joys, divides our griefs and whose honesty is inviolable.
- One who understands our silence.
- Friends are like good health: you don't realize what a gift they are until you lose them. Prosperity begets friends; adversity proves them. Friends do their knocking before they enter, instead of after they leave.

C. S. Lewis was someone who deeply understood and appreciated friendship. He knew how vital it was, but also how it gets forged: 'Friendship is unnecessary, like philosophy, like art . . . It has no survival value; rather it is one of those things which give value to survival.'[4]

How true this is for those in the cave. But Lewis's most famous insight on the subject is even more relevant: 'Friendship is born at that moment when one person says to another, "What! You, too? I thought I was the only one." '[5]

This is never truer than when you discover others in the black dog cave. Their cave experiences will never be identical, of course. But you will share a common awareness of cave life. That brings the chance, at last, of a genuine connection. It is no wonder, then, that the comedian turned professional psychologist, Ruby Wax, often refers to those who have lived in the cave as 'my people'. She suffered terribly herself, which is what motivated her academic pursuits as a mature student.

Getting to know others in a similar boat is almost liberating by itself.

Sometimes, all it takes is comparing notes on which depression metaphors resonate most. Or it is the sense of an empathetic listener or fellow-traveller. But what is certain, again and again, is the sense that one degree of isolation has been removed. We are no longer alone.

That is why my favourite friendship definition submitted to that newspaper is this one:

- A friend is the first person who walks in when the whole world [or, dare I say it, even the church] walks out.

That, more than anything else, is what cave-dwellers yearn for.

## 4. THE WEIGHT

King David simply could not sleep. Wide-eyed while the city snored, trying to control his pumping heart and cold sweat. He couldn't explain it. Or perhaps, to be more accurate, he wouldn't explain it. He just couldn't bear it:

> When I kept silent,
>     my bones wasted away
>     through my groaning all day long.
> For day and night
>     your hand was heavy on me;
> my strength was sapped
>     as in the heat of summer.
> (Psalm 32:3–4)

In his heart of hearts, of course, he knew perfectly well what it meant. He understood why he felt so terrible. He had done wrong. Yes, the great king of Israel himself – he had sinned. He tried to get away with it, perhaps because he was the king. After all, it would never do to let the people know that their esteemed leader had feet of clay.

But he could not hide it indefinitely – not from himself, and certainly not from the God who searches all our hearts. He does not reveal the nature of the sin that was plaguing his conscience this time (he would do so for Psalm 51, of course). But that is hardly the point. What matters here is how it affected his relationship with God, as the next verse makes clear:

> Then I acknowledged my sin to you
> > and did not cover up my iniquity.
> I said, 'I will confess
> > my transgressions to the LORD.'
> And you forgave
> > the guilt of my sin.
> (Psalm 32:5)

The problem with genuine guilt, the reason why we conceal it, is our fear of the consequences when it is discovered. How will others react? What will happen to me? How astonishing, therefore, for David to find this response from the God he was fleeing: 'You forgave the guilt of my sin.' Confession of his guilt was the only remedy for David's agony at that moment.

Discerning the relationship between guilt and depression would be hard enough, were it not for the added complication of the phenomenon of shame. The three can get confused

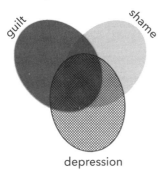

and blurred. There is naturally overlap (see the diagram), but serious problems can arise if they are treated in the same way. I have found that my depression has fed off the sense of my own guilt and shame, which is why I have needed to probe their relationship to mental health.

## The pain of genuine guilt

It is vital to start here, although I am all too aware of how treacherous the subject is in the quagmire of depression. So it is *imperative* that this section is not read in isolation from the next one. It will become clear why, but for now, simply note that guilt gets intertwined with depression. They are not identical – many who *are* guilty may not *feel* guilty, nor will they inevitably experience depression. Yet, as this diagram illustrates, the reality of guilt can generate depressive experiences. But this interconnection is sensitive and potentially destructive. Any clumsy probing or thoughtless mishandling of this issue can be devastating.

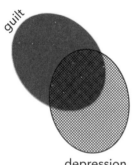

Of course, we cannot deny our lack of perfection, regardless of our mental health. None of us leads lives of which we can be entirely proud. All have skeletons in the cupboard – all of us – thoughts, words and deeds which reveal the reality that we follow 'the devices and desires of our own hearts' (as the old prayer book vividly put it[1]). We live in God's world as if it were our own. No other explanation does justice to the chaos and brokenness all around us that gets reported in the daily news.

No amount of psychobabble or New Age wishful thinking can wash away reality. No amount of relativizing morality can wipe slates clean, as if good and evil were simply human constructs. That's far too simplistic. More than that, it is cruel: it fails to take injustice and victimhood seriously. We all have a tainted past and, based on our track records, we will have a tainted future too. We all have people we let down, promises we failed to keep, loved ones we hurt. Having taken many funerals over the years, I have lost count of the times a recently deceased person is described as one 'who never did any harm'. I just don't believe it. Because I know myself.

Yet there is a specific and paradoxical pressure on those in pastoral ministry. We are no less (or more) broken, sinful or guilty than anyone else. Yet the New Testament expectations could not be clearer. Quite apart from the necessary qualifications for teaching and leadership, the apostle Paul repeatedly says we should be 'worthy of full respect' and of 'good reputation' (1 Timothy 3:4–8; Titus 2:2); 'blameless' or 'free from accusation' (1 Timothy 3:10; Titus 1:6); 'self-controlled' and 'faithful' (1 Timothy 3:2, 9; Titus 1:8–9). That is just the start of it – the expectations on church leaders are nothing if not demanding. Now, at one level, nothing here is unique to leaders. All who trust in Christ should pursue these virtues. Yet, as leaders, our own discipleship is inevitably much more visible.

No wonder, then, that those of us in ministry find it harder to acknowledge our flaws and failings. We feel torn in two. The great weight of our sin makes us groan, and yet God's high standards and our people's expectations make us reluctant to acknowledge that weight. We are anxious about how our leadership status might be affected – after all, we are *meant* to have a good reputation. Our consciences prick and prod us, but we cannot bear the weight. As if to compensate for the guilt or alleviate the pain, futile though it so obviously is, we drive ourselves even harder. We begin to feel that unless we are overworking, we are somehow failing God. This only serves to make matters much worse. It is, in fact, a form of psychological self-harm.

David's imagery of energy-sapping heat is apt. Even though only 35 km (about 22 miles) from the equator, we noticed, over the four years living in Kampala, that it seldom became too hot. But on those rare occasions when temperatures soared, it felt as if the earth's gravity had doubled. Every single movement became an effort. We would think twice before embarking on anything strenuous. I do remember, though, that many of my students would complain about it far more than us foreigners!

Guilt saps energy like the sun's heat – but without the daily reprieve of dusk and night. As David said, this weight brings groaning 'day and night'. Relief seems unattainable. Despair sets in. It will perhaps be obvious here that these physical symptoms and emotional responses are not so different from those of depression, mentioned in chapter 2. What's more, I suspect that for those in Christian leadership, genuine guilt for sin can feel even worse, simply because of the expectations on us. If we have any self-awareness at all, an acknowledgment of hypocrisy is rarely far from the surface.

It may even be that a specific act of wrongdoing hangs over us, as it famously did for Shakespeare's Lady Macbeth. She walks and speaks in her sleep, hallucinating the blood spatter on her hands from assassinating King Duncan. In desperation to be clean, physically and morally, she wrings her hands. It is a wretched moment in a bleak play.

But whether we are citizens or kings, preachers or prisoners, makes little difference. None of us can flee from the God who exists. Each of us must come clean before him to have any hope of being made clean by him.

Here is David again, this time with even greater detail of his guilt's physical symptoms:

LORD, do not rebuke me in your anger
    or discipline me in your wrath.
Your arrows have pierced me,
    and your hand has come down on me.
Because of your wrath there is no health in my body;
    there is no soundness in my bones because of my sin.
My guilt has overwhelmed me
    like a burden too heavy to bear.
My wounds fester and are loathsome
    because of my sinful folly.
I am bowed down and brought very low;
    all day long I go about mourning.
My back is filled with searing pain;
    there is no health in my body.
I am feeble and utterly crushed;
    I groan in anguish of heart.
All my longings lie open before you, Lord:
    my sighing is not hidden from you.
My heart pounds, my strength fails me;
    even the light has gone from my eyes.
(Psalm 38:1–10)

Perhaps it seems alarming for David to insist that it is God who makes him feel this way. He insists that God's arrows and anger cause this overwhelming burden. But David knows he takes no malicious pleasure in this – it seems the only means by which a resistant conscience can be aroused to come to him in confession. So, just as with Psalm 32, David groans in his guilt and resistance to God, until he turns back to him.

The psalm then continues for ten more verses. But here in the final verses, David can only cast himself on God's mercy in the hope of receiving it:

LORD, do not forsake me;
    do not be far from me, my God.
Come quickly to help me,
    my Lord and my Saviour.
(Psalm 38:21–22)

He does not receive the assurance of forgiveness quite as speedily as he had done in Psalm 32. But the hints of God's mercy are there, nevertheless. For the God to whom he now runs is not just Lord; he is also Saviour: a saviour who specializes in rescuing, and cleansing, sinners.

But this is where it gets complicated.

## Where guilt and depression meet

Depression does not somehow excuse sin. It may explain wrongdoing, but it cannot legitimize it. This may seem an unnecessary point, but the affliction can sometimes breed a victim mentality that gets used to excuse, and even justify, any behaviour. For it is hard to deny that depression and anxiety, as well as other forms of mental illness, can lead to self-centredness. I have been all too aware of this over the last decade or so. I can go into lockdown mode and focus exclusively on my own needs and wants. Those who are closest to me, particularly Rachel and the children, bear the brunt. When the despair has felt so overwhelming, I have lashed out in the most horrible ways against those within firing range. In fact, in my more discreditable moments, I mask my wants as needs. This is not unique to depressives, of course. We all do it. Our hearts easily deceive us, as the prophet Jeremiah knew only too well (Jeremiah 17:9).

Yet, at the same time, there is a fine line between culpable self-centredness and the effort required simply to keep going.

It is not always easy to distinguish between our guilt and our depression. If it is tricky for a sufferer to work that out, it is impossible for those who don't battle it. Beware of trying to prise the two apart. On the odd occasion when someone tried to do so, it was shattering. For it is sometimes all we can do to hold everything together internally to avoid a nervous collapse.

Perhaps it helps to see it as akin to someone having a panic attack in deep water. The terrified swimmer thrashes about, oblivious to how much harder this makes it for a lifesaver. I suppose you could call that selfish and thoughtless. I prefer to call it the natural result of fear and the survival instinct (however misguided the thrashing about might be). In panic, the person does what comes instinctively to keep his or her head above water. To calm down enough to trust the rescuer takes superhuman presence of mind.

So I wonder if there needs to be greater empathetic understanding here. It is striking that in the Anglican confession liturgy, the congregation prays these words:

Almighty God, our heavenly Father,
we have sinned against you
and against our neighbour
in thought and word and deed,
through negligence, through weakness,
through our own deliberate fault.

Notice the distinction between three different causes: negligence, weakness, deliberate fault. As one friend wondered aloud to me, perhaps people focus too much on deliberate fault, without factoring in our falling through weaknesses. For there is little doubt that depression debilitates and weakens.

People can be so quick to blame and condemn, when we crave and need forgiveness and healing.

There is a far worse complicating factor, however. Few outside the cave realize it even exists, but it is one of the primary reasons why blame and condemnation are lethal. This is the inadequacy and wretchedness that the black dog induces in the *guise* of guilt. It thrives on this, in fact. So it is highly likely that a depressed person feels overwhelmed by a guilt that has no basis in reality whatsoever.

## The curse of imagined guilt

The mind is a great mystery. It has extraordinary powers, of which scientists can comprehend only a tiny fraction. So, for example, it can dupe someone into believing there are physical symptoms where none exists. My maternal grandfather died when I was twelve. He was a remarkable man in so many ways, and even then, I revered, rather than knew, him, probably because he was never quite able to relate to young children!

But some time before his death, part of his leg was amputated. Such radical intervention is only performed when necessary, but he had been in considerable pain before the operation. Afterwards, the strangest thing happened. The cause of his pain had disappeared, but the sensation of his pain did not. He was afflicted by so-called 'phantom pains', unfortunately a common repercussion of amputation. It sounds absurd – and it is – he could see that his lower leg had gone, yet still it throbbed.

Similarly, a depressed mind can convince us of a kind of 'phantom guilt', which might feel just like genuine guilt but is different (see the diagram opposite). Perhaps like its physical equivalent, it occupies a mental space where the sensation of

genuine guilt existed previously.
Or it may have transferred that
sensation to the general experience of depression, such that it
feels like guilt but without any
grounds. So, even though guilt
finds a remedy in divine forgiveness, as we will see, the darkness
and even despair that it brings
are much harder to deal with. As

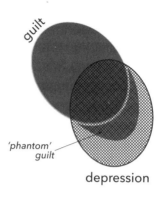

for a remedy for 'phantom guilt', that is a different problem
altogether.

### Not a matter of mistaken guilt . . .

I am not referring here to *mistaken* feelings of guilt – a bad
conscience derived from actions that one falsely believes to
be wrong. One of the gravest responsibilities for a spiritual
leader is teaching the difference between freedom and
holiness. Isaiah, for one, rebuked religious leaders for their
cruel insistence on neutral, or even good, things being sinful,
while conversely claiming that genuine sins are no such
thing:

> Woe to those who call evil good
>     and good evil,
> who put darkness for light
>     and light for darkness,
> who put bitter for sweet
>     and sweet for bitter.
> (Isaiah 5:20)

Centuries later, the problem persisted, as Jesus' rebukes of
the Pharisees suggests (Matthew 23). This is why faithful

and careful teaching of the Scriptures by gospel-shaped ministers is crucial. What relief it is to be shown from the Bible that a 'sin' you feel terrible about is in fact no such thing.

### Not a matter of feeling unforgivable . . .

Another necessary distinction is between phantom guilt and the inability to forgive oneself. That can occur because one's guilt for a specific action persists after knowing, and even believing in, divine forgiveness. Some diagnose a deep-rooted pride behind this, because overly high self-esteem can be so severely dented that it results in self-recrimination.

But others should not be too quick to latch on to this kind of diagnosis. It is too easy, too pat, and potentially crippling. The diagnosis has a certain logic to it, of course, so it is easy to see how someone might attempt to guide a depressed person into rooting out concealed pride. But that is potentially disastrous. This is because it is partly related to shame, which we will come to. It could also be related to entirely unrealistic expectations of self and the world, which make failure inevitable. This is not so much pride as its opposite.

### . . . But a dislocated sensation of guilt

Instead, I'm talking about a lingering *sensation* of guilt. This is a black dog speciality. It gets triggered in so many ways. It might start with genuine wrongdoing, but its significance is blown out of proportion by mentally rewinding the moment over and over. We all know the phenomenon, I'm sure, whereby insignificant issues progressively gain scale in the mind.

Most of us press the mental rewind button to review an argument or conflict in which we fared badly and – surprise,

surprise – our performance vastly improves second time around! We come out with those great zingers that silence the opposition once and for all. Sadly, it's all in the mind, and it's far too late. Still, we rarely fail to come out looking much better in the reruns.

Unless we're depressed.

Then the reruns become far less about massaging a bruised ego, and more about digging oneself deeper into the cave. Any negative comment or accusation, especially if it has substance, begins its corrosive work. The offending conversation gets repeated, the words and motives of the other person get distorted, the guilt becomes ever more burdensome. I'm left buckling under the weight.

Or it could be the awareness of how my depression is affecting those closest to me, like my family or closest friends. For example, I might become completely uncommunicative when all they need is some assurance. Looking back at those moments of apparent passivity, I can honestly say that, inside, the brain blizzard was so great that I couldn't even get a word out. That is the nature of the affliction. Yet, simultaneously, I'm left horribly aware of my failure to help them.

Then there are the times when there is no obvious basis at all. That is the worst – so unsettling and disorienting. I stand in the dock, and I plead guilty to all charges, even when the charge sheet is blank. I'm convinced that 'I'm going down' as soon as the imaginary judge bangs the gavel. It's absurd. It's irrational.

At one level, this phenomenon is not the exclusive preserve of those fighting depression, nor is the black dog the only prosecutor. For, from Genesis 3 onwards, we all have an opponent who delights to rub our noses in our guilt – false or genuine. The devil's name, Satan, actually means 'accuser' or 'adversary' (see Psalm 109:6; Zechariah 3:1–2). He is also the 'father of lies' (John 8:44; 2 Corinthians 11:14). So few things delight him more than the anguish of Christians. He is a consummate bully. He brutally exploits mental illness as well. But I am acutely conscious of how risky this language is, because we must be wary of ascribing to the devil more power than he actually has. He is a defeated enemy.

But, for a depressed person, this awareness of guilt may be a constant. I sometimes experience it as a deep-seated dread, relentless like the background hum on spaceships in science fiction movies. It can be termed anxiety in that respect, but specifically an anxiety about the moral status of guilt (perhaps the depression itself can feel like a punishment), which grounds the nagging fear of being 'discovered'. Yet, much of the time, there is nothing to discover.

A common apprehension when going through airport security scanners is feeling sure you are going to get caught. You might even feel embarrassment and dread . . . even though there is absolutely nothing to hide. And even if you do set off the bleeper, it adds only a minute or two to the process. It is totally irrational. But then so is black dog guilt. It sometimes lasts for whole days at a time. From my first conscious thoughts on waking, right up until my head hits the pillow and I doze off, the background hum is there. Yet, cruelly, there is no true basis for this. It is phantom guilt.

It makes a big difference if friends and loved ones can begin to grasp this.

## When 'helping' hurts

Those who battle with depression are utterly dependent on those around them, and yet, unfortunately, they are also vulnerable to them. Despite the best intentions, thoughtless words or challenges can exacerbate rather than relieve the pain. Matters of sin and guilt are especially precarious, because of the strong temptation to diagnose the root causes of the suffering.

Let us return to Psalm 38 for a moment and consider the verses I omitted. David continues to cry out to God for rescue. But now, instead of relief from his guilt, he seeks rescue from his 'enemies':

> My friends and companions avoid me because
>     of my wounds;
>   my neighbours stay far away.
> Those who want to kill me set their traps,
>   those who would harm me talk of my ruin;
>   all day long they scheme and lie.
> I am like the deaf, who cannot hear,
>   like the mute, who cannot speak;
> I have become like one who does not hear,
>   whose mouth can offer no reply.
> LORD, I wait for you;
>   you will answer, Lord my God.
> For I said, 'Do not let them gloat
>   or exalt themselves over me when my feet slip.'
> For I am about to fall,
>   and my pain is ever with me.
> I confess my iniquity;
>   I am troubled by my sin.
> Many have become my enemies without cause;
>   those who hate me without reason are numerous.
> Those who repay my good with evil
>   lodge accusations against me,
>   though I seek only to do what is good.
> (Psalm 38:11–20)

It is hard to know here whether David speaks literally or metaphorically. As Israel's anointed king, he certainly had lethal enemies, both before and after his enthronement. So it is entirely plausible that they really are seeking to kill him. Whichever it is, he feels isolated and vulnerable, because people are kicking him when he is down. Friends abandon him in his pain; opponents take advantage of his pain.

Human nature hasn't changed much. It is sometimes said that the church is the only army that shoots its own wounded. When people are in difficulty, their struggle may well manifest itself in some public outburst perhaps or a moral failing. Yet, all too often, the response from believers is to pounce on that wrongdoing, without addressing the underlying problem. As if the struggler's sense of guilt wasn't strong enough already.

So, after his pleading with God in the first ten verses of Psalm 38, David now cries for rescue:

> For I said, 'Do not let them gloat
>    or exalt themselves over me when my feet slip.'
> For I am about to fall,
>    and my pain is ever with me.
> (verses 16–17)

It is interesting, therefore, to see the similarity of David's experience to that of Job. David never denies his own wrongdoing – 38:18 reinforces his confession. But he knows how his suffering far exceeds what is directly deserved. When he does try to do the right thing, however haltingly, he suffers even more (38:20). So he longs for God to put things right. Just as Job did.

### The sin equation

Job's situation was not identical to David's, of course. David's friends desert him because they appear unable to cope with his pain. Job's four friends, on the other hand – his so-called 'comforters' – do stick with him. Three of them get it right. To begin with.

> When they saw him from a distance, they could hardly recognise him; they began to weep aloud, and they tore their robes and sprinkled dust on their heads. Then they sat on the ground with him for seven days and seven nights. No one said a word to him, because they saw how great his suffering was. (Job 2:12–13)

Then they make their first error: they open their mouths! They initially intend to console Job, but they end up accusing him. Each tries to prod Job into a confession. They assume that the extremity of his suffering could *only* be explained by some appalling, but concealed, transgression. To illustrate, here is one of the four, Zophar:

> You say to God, 'My beliefs are flawless
>     and I am pure in your sight.'
> Oh, how I wish that God would speak,
>     that he would open his lips against you
> and disclose to you the secrets of wisdom,
>     for true wisdom has two sides.
>     Know this: God has even forgotten some of your sin.
> (Job 11:4–6)

Zophar follows the logic of what we now recognize as the Hindu notion of karma, a cosmic law whereby the universe determines that each of us gets what we deserve. If I sin, I suffer (see the diagram). As Psalms 32 and 38 illustrate,

my sin ➡ I suffer

genuine guilt does indeed lead to suffering, whether physically, mentally or spiritually.

The great irony is that, by the close of the book of Job, God does indeed speak. But he does so in order to vindicate Job and rebuke his friends. Zophar has been far too simplistic. Like his fellow 'comforters', he assumes the world is neat, tidy and, above all, logical. He presumes that if Job is suffering, it is because there are secret sins that Job has concealed. It matters little that he cannot identify them himself – he's merely concealing them from himself in that case. For, in this kind of world, suffering must *always* be a punishment. It is logical. How else to explain pain in a world ruled by a God who is sovereign and just?

Now, it is true. There *are* instances of this in the Bible. It may simply be the natural consequences of my actions, or equally, the result of God 'handing us over' to those consequences (as the apostle Paul puts it in Romans 1:18–32). In fact, because of his apostolic insight, Paul discerns that it is the Corinthians' sinful behaviour at the Lord's Supper which results in their declining health, or worse (1 Corinthians 11:29–30).

### Reversing the equation?

So, if Paul can do that, can we? Can we assume that the equation between sin and suffering is reversible (see the diagram)? If individuals are suffering, *must* the cause always be their sin?

That is certainly how a karmic worldview works. If I have a car accident, or my children get sick, or I battle with depression, it must be because of some terrible deed, whether in this life or (in the Hindu worldview) in a previous life. It is simple retribution.

But, while there is a logic to it, there is also a brutality and an oppressiveness. It hardly fosters genuine charity or compassion, since somebody else's suffering is deserved. They *deserve* to be left alone to stew in their pain, self-pity and misery.

But life is not so straightforward, or cruel, and the Judeo-Christian worldview of the Bible profoundly rejects karmic causality. Thankfully. Job knew that his sin was nothing like as serious as to deserve such pain. He instinctively understood that suffering has several possible causes (see the diagram). We can suffer because of the selfishness and sin of others, whether it is directed against us or not. In fact, the majority of stories in daily news bulletins could be grouped under this category, from the multinational right down to the neighbourhood.

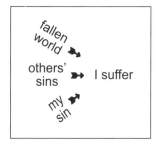

Then there are the afflictions for which others are less blameworthy: natural disasters or diseases (apart from those that result from lifestyles or behaviours). We put these down to simple bad luck, to being in the wrong place at the wrong time. There seems no rhyme or reason behind it. This genuinely *is* innocent suffering. Not because anyone is entirely innocent. None of us can claim that. But because our suffering is *not* deserved.

This was the great conviction behind the book of Job. For Job resolutely clings to the point, despite the comforters. And God proves him right in the end (despite, frustratingly, never granting him an alternative explanation for his pain):

> After the LORD had said these things to Job, he said to Eliphaz
> the Temanite, 'I am angry with you and your two friends,

because you have not spoken the truth about me, as my servant Job has. So now take seven bulls and seven rams and go to my servant Job and sacrifice a burnt offering for yourselves. My servant Job will pray for you, and I will accept his prayer and not deal with you according to your folly. You have not spoken the truth about me, as my servant Job has.'

(Job 42:7–8)

## The precision of gospel remedies

A wonder of the Christian message is its diametrically opposed alternative to the karmic worldview. There is an escape from guilt. Bono wrote a beautifully simple song called 'Grace' which makes this contrast explicit. Playing on the fact that it is a girl's name as well as a wonderful truth, he sings,

> She's got the time to talk
> She travels outside of karma
> . . .
> Because Grace makes beauty
> Out of ugly things.[2]

Grace is counter-intuitive, illogical, overwhelming. Thank God. It is a word that captures the glorious absurdity of *not* being given what we deserve, while simultaneously being granted what we *don't* deserve. Paul spells it out perfectly in 1 Corinthians:

> God was reconciling the world to himself in Christ, not counting people's sins against them. And he has committed to us the message of reconciliation . . . God made him who

had no sin to be sin for us, so that in him we might become
the righteousness of God.
(2 Corinthians 5:19–21)

This can't be earned, only received. It is never deserved, only
enjoyed. It is the only hope for the guilty. It is grounds for all
hope and lasting joy. All because of what Christ has done at
the cross to deal with our guilt once and for all. The divine
grace of the Christian gospel is unique.

Philip Yancey tells a story from a British conference on
comparative religion, at which delegates were discussing
what, if anything, was unique about Christianity. Claims to
incarnation and resurrection were found in other worldviews,
so they did not qualify. C. S. Lewis wandered into the room:
'"What's the rumpus about?" he asked, and heard in reply
that his colleagues were discussing Christianity's unique
contribution among world religions. Lewis responded, "Oh,
that's easy. It's grace."'[3]

After further discussion, the delegates agreed with him.
There was indeed something extraordinary, scandalous even,
about Christian grace. The very notion that God would freely
grant liberation from our guilt and lack of fidelity to him is
not found anywhere else. It is indeed scandalous – but only
for those who presume that God expects us to slave away to
earn his favour. For those who have faced up to the futility of
that, this invasion of grace brings astonishing relief and joy
(see the diagram).

John Bunyan described the experience vividly in *The Pilgrim's Progress*:

> Now I saw in my dream, that the highway up which CHRISTIAN was to go was fenced on either side with a wall; and that wall was called 'Salvation'.
>
> In that day shall this song be sung in the land of Judah; We have a strong city; salvation will *God* appoint *for* walls and bulwarks. (Isaiah 26:1)
>
> Up this way, therefore, did burdened CHRISTIAN run; but not without great difficulty, because of the load on his back.
>
> He ran thus till he came at a place somewhat ascending; and upon that place stood a Cross, and a little below, in the bottom, a sepulchre. So I saw in my dream, that just as CHRISTIAN came up to the cross, his burden loosed from off his shoulders, and fell from off his back, and began to tumble; and so continued to do till it came to the mouth of the sepulchre, where it fell in, and I saw it no more.
>
> Then was CHRISTIAN glad and lightsome, and said, with a merry heart,
>
> 'He hath given me rest by his sorrow, And life by his death.'
>
> Then he stood still awhile to look and wonder; for it was very surprising to him, that the sight of the cross should thus ease him of his burden. He looked therefore, and looked again, even till the springs that were in his head sent the waters down his cheeks.[4]

Such is the power of divine grace. And a depressed person needs to hear and relish it as much as any other. In fact, we can never hear it enough. Christ lifts the weight of guilt from our shoulders.

I look back over the years with such gratitude for those who taught and showed me that grace. It changed my life. I had been the kind of person who didn't especially mind talking about God-stuff, but would never have given much thought or credence to Jesus. 'God' was a suitably vague concept, into which one could import whatever agendas or interests one liked. 'Jesus' was far too specific, with much less room for the whims of creativity. So it was disquieting, to say the least, to attend a Lent talks series, during the last February at secondary school, led by someone very comfortable with talking about Jesus. More than that, he implied he knew him personally. Most significant of all, though, was what he explained – that this reconciliation with God won by Christ brought the wonder of forgiveness. I don't remember much else about those few days – and it probably took weeks, if not months, for it all to sink in fully. But I do clearly recall a sense of open-mouthed amazement that Jesus was in the forgiveness business (as opposed to the pull-your-socks-up-and-be-good religion business). For various reasons, the timing of these talks was perfect. I was receptive and profoundly relieved to hear them. As I say, they changed my life for ever.

Yet this was no 'cure' for, let alone prevention of, my mental health problems. Jesus never promised ease or comfort in this life. As it happened, I only became aware of these challenges long after I first accepted that revolutionary grace for myself. It is strangely comforting, therefore, that Bunyan puts this moment near the start of *The Pilgrim's Progress*, long before Christian and Hopeful find themselves in Giant Despair's castle. That shows great pastoral wisdom as well as theological insight.

So it is crucial to recognize that well-intentioned presentations of this gospel liberation may not have the hoped-for result. It may even leave sufferers feeling *more* wretched. This is because for a depressed person, and indeed for many even in the West today, guilt is not the only problem. There is another, more extensive, ailment, on which the message of forgiveness has little or no impact.

We must now turn to the problem of shame.

## 5. THE INVISIBILITY CLOAK

Looking back, my job at a busy London church would have seemed utterly improbable thirty years earlier.

At school, I recoiled from doing anything in public. Even classroom discussions were daunting. The anticipation of formal public speaking would have sent me scuttling for the exit. Even more hair-raising was the prospect of performing music in public.

I love music and was very involved at school, though not to a very high standard. This is not false modesty. It was manifestly clear to me at that time, because I was surrounded by some very gifted friends who are now well-established professionals in the classical music world. I sang in the school choir, which took the craft of singing seriously – we went on international tours and all had individual singing lessons paid for by the choral foundation. Consequently, we were each expected to enter the annual singing competition. That was terrifying. After I was done, I remember my tutor remarking wryly that I was the only one who remembered to bring his music with him. But the truth was, there was no way I was going to stand on a bare stage without any shields at all. I went back to my boarding house immediately after it was over, awkward, embarrassed and still trembling.

Yet, for the last twenty-five years, I have done a job that requires me to be a public figure, albeit on a small scale. I never sing in public, of course. But I do most other things, including fulfilling the occasional requirement of deliberately making a fool of myself (in staff Christmas plays or embarrassing turns at retreats and camps). I have changed considerably.

One thing clearly hasn't, though. That is the terror of exposure. It's not so much a question of being in public as the fear of being laid bare in public. It is the latent fear of being an imposter, making it only a matter of time before the fraud is brought to light.

Christian ministry is public. How can it not be? At its heart, it is a matter of inspiring vibrant community life centred on Christ. It can never – must never – be reduced to concepts or precepts, truth claims or group gatherings. So ministry can never be private. We put ourselves 'out there', with what can appear to be a breathtaking audacity. We stand up week by week, in front of countless others, with a peculiar confidence to lead them in the ways of God. Of course, if we take that seriously, most of us do so in fear and trembling.

Being on the ministry team in a large, central London church meant that we might regularly have 2,000 or more on a Sunday, people listening to our every word in hushed expectancy and hunger to learn. But, of course, the audience size is immaterial. A small rural fellowship, perhaps, or a fellowship hemmed in by a hostile majority culture, will have the same effect. We find ourselves, and are expected to function, as public figures. That means others have a sense of ownership. I become *somebody's* pastor. I work (and perhaps even exist) to serve *them*. But, more alarmingly, I am exposed: to public scrutiny, to public appraisal, even to public disdain. We naturally expect our politicians to face that and can only assume they have prepared for it. Perhaps foolishly, I hadn't really factored it in at all when I started training for church ministry. It's definitely a reality now, though!

So perhaps it was never going to be that difficult to face up to what (for me) is the most devastating aspect of depression: the shame. As already mentioned, I was knocked back by the first awareness of it on a wintry Berlin afternoon. And it has never gone away.

## The crisis of personhood

Shame is an insidious affliction. It is concealed, buried deep within consciousness, but with crippling effects. It compounds the isolation that depression instils, giving it a compelling justification. In contrast to guilt, which provokes a fear of the discovery of *what I have done*, shame generates a fear of the discovery of *who I am*. It is all-encompassing. But it has taken me time to understand why. It took full immersion into a sizeable list of books on the subject before it clicked into place.

One reason is the Western presumption that shame is not 'our' issue.[1] Perhaps this blind spot derived from taking to heart Ruth Benedict's now largely discredited distinction in 1946 between the United States' *guilt culture* and Japan's *shame culture*.[2] Despite her implication that shame is a less relevant concept for Westerners, the truth is that shame and guilt are too closely intertwined to be aided by unhelpful reductionisms. If Benedict's terms have any value today, some have suggested using 'guilt-oriented' and 'shame-oriented' to describe cultures instead. What does seem to be taking place is a shift in Western cultures towards being more shame-aware than they have been, perhaps, since the Reformation.

Be that as it may, the fact remains that it is a much more prevalent issue in our communities than we realize. Many languish in silence, lacking both the vocabulary and sympathy for the pain. What is true in wider society is inevitably true within churches. Yet I cannot recall a single sermon that engaged with it! To be fair, I have not preached one either (though that will now change). If my own experience is anything to go by, this is devastating, and profoundly undermines the witness of the church for reasons that will become clear.

## Features of shame

But what precisely are we talking about here? Two clarifications will help.

We first must distinguish between good and bad shame, a distinction dating at least as far back as Homer's Greece.[3]

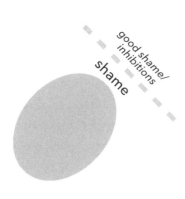

'Good shame' is essentially a healthy self-awareness that cultivates the modesty appropriate to a finite human being (see the diagram). It prevents us from overstepping the mark, into atrocity or hubris. Good shame holds us back from actions of which we ought to be ashamed. Thus, in Homer's *Iliad*, the god Apollo condemned Achilles for his appalling treatment of the Trojan Hector's body:

The man has lost all mercy;
he has no shame – that gift that hinders mortals
but helps them too.
. . . Let him take care,
or, brave as he is, we gods will turn against him,
seeing him outrage the insensate earth![4]

Achilles has ignored the moral codes at the heart of the universe – his actions would have grave consequences for him. With enough shame, he would never have done this. While we no longer live in the mythological world of demigods and heroes, this kind of shame is arguably in woefully short supply today.

Now, this is clearly far removed from the corrosive affliction that I am considering here. Good shame is related to modesty, so it provides protection. It keeps us operating within the bounds of appropriate and healthy social norms, and so protects us from showing disrespect, and worse, to others (especially the vulnerable). Bad shame never does. Bad shame cripples and crushes us.

The second clarification comes from dissecting the relationship between shame and guilt, which I alluded to in the first chapter. Glynn Harrison is a friend who was Professor of Psychiatry at Bristol University. He sums it up perfectly:

As guilt is the emotion linked to specific wrongs I commit, shame is the emotion that springs from *being the kind of person that does that sort of thing*. Shame, indeed, is the emotion of inferiority . . . But shame isn't always linked to moral culpability and guilt. There were many other moments of shame in my childhood (as there probably were in yours) that had nothing to do with wrongdoing.[5]

Guilt is the consequence of *doing* bad, while shame is the response to *being* – or at least *feeling* – bad.

At last, I understood my headlong rush for concealment, that inexplicable longing for what could best be described as an 'invisibility cloak'. I was profoundly ashamed of who I was. This was undoubtedly one of the fuels for depression's fire (see the diagram).

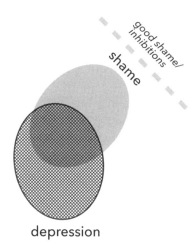

depression

Now, Harry Potter was not the first to make use of one of these miraculous articles, though J. K. Rowling can certainly take credit for reviving their popularity. They crop up in myths and legends of all sorts, including those of the ancient Greeks, Celts and Norse. Harry resorts to his when some undercover snooping is in order, when invisibility is the only means of discovering the enemy's conspiracies. It is a very useful device indeed – especially for an author who can't think of an alternative method for quickly revealing important information!

My longing for one had no such clandestine motive. I wasn't on some quest of discovery. Instead, I dreaded becoming 'a discovery'.

The sense would swell when in large groups, perhaps in the coffee time after church or at a large family gathering. Strangely, it didn't seem to make much difference whether the crowd was familiar or unknown. Nor was it something I could articulate. I just knew I would get increasingly agitated, and wanted to be a million miles away. I would far rather be at home with a good book and U2 or Schubert. Or, if being away was not possible, then an invisibility cloak would be the answer! I could be present as requested, but not have to interact about myself. It wasn't a problem to talk to others about their lives and concerns; I just wanted to avoid reciprocal enquiries. Even a question as anodyne and cursory as 'How are you?' can feel like a threat.

Of course, this could simply be put down to a natural tendency towards introversion. I am sceptical of tight psychological categorizations, because they rarely avoid reductionism, especially in the wrong hands. But they do have a place in identifying temperaments and differences from others. So, in the Myers-Briggs scheme, I come out as clearly 'introverted' in contrast to 'extroverted'. There is no doubt that I tend to be energized by time away from others. That does not mean wanting to avoid people (which is how introversion is sometimes misconstrued). I need others – and struggle with extended periods without human interaction. That is the difference between solitude and isolation: the former is necessary for healthy living because it energizes and replenishes; the latter cripples and desiccates us because we were not wired by our Creator for loneliness. I positively relish solitude, but dread isolation.

The craving for an invisibility cloak goes far beyond normal, healthy introversion. If guilt leaves us with a fear of the consequences (such as punishment), shame leaves us with a terror of exposure. That is what generates the desire to cover up and remain undisturbed. It is precisely because exposure is the greatest threat for the shamed that nakedness is such a potent symbol for it. This is not the supposedly alluring nudity of the pornographic, but the cowering nakedness of the vulnerable. The shamed don't just want clothes; they want total invisibility.

Quite where these feelings originate is not so straightforward.

## Seeds for shame

It is a perfectly natural question, I suppose. When a friend battles depression, the first instinct is to wonder why. This needn't be motivated by the blame agenda of Job's comforters, but, at its best, may well derive from a desire to understand. It's almost as instinctive as asking 'What sort?' on hearing that someone has been diagnosed with cancer.

If only mental illness were so straightforward! An obvious cause might then have obvious treatments. Yet the shame that accompanies depression is one of its more mysterious elements.

Thankfully, one thing was clear to me. I realized that my family did not lie at its roots. I have never experienced anything other than the strongest acceptance and value from my parents – I have always been, and remain, secure in their love for me. Of course, we have our differences and quibbles; we can wind each other up like clockwork. Which family doesn't? But this doesn't change the deeper reality, and for that, my gratitude and affection have no bounds. Over the years of my ministry, I have heard from too many who never knew such foundations, and it has been heartbreaking. Lack of parental security as children accounts for a huge range of pastoral problems, long into adulthood.

Likewise, my wife and children cannot be its cause either, for at least two reasons. One is that the experience long predates marriage and fatherhood. Everyone contributes his or her own baggage to a marriage, and I certainly had mine! Second, the reality of their love has never been in doubt. Thank God and them.

But this makes the shame, and depression (for that matter), even more of a mystery.

It is important to reiterate the contrast with guilt. For shame derives not simply from things we do (and genuine guilt can feed the shame), but also from the things done to us. This explains why the abused, bullied or abandoned can all feel shame, as the diagram illustrates. A perverse logic coils around our perceptions, convincing us that whatever we suffered can *only* have been caused by personal deficiency or just deserts.

An extreme case might be a child put up for adoption in infancy. Regardless of her parents' circumstances or social pressures, it seems impossible to resist finding root causes in her own failings and personality. No other explanation seems to make sense of the abandonment.

Bullying and abuse rob their victims of a sense of autonomy and agency, compounding it with feelings of blameworthiness. Of course, that is profoundly unjust. The victim of another's abuse or aggression can *never* be held responsible for them. Yet, as Curt Thompson explains, that self-blame comes from 'a sense of "there being something wrong" with me or of "not being enough," and therefore exudes the aroma of being unable or powerless to change one's condition or circumstances'.[6] The longer this continues, the harder it is to escape its clutches. This leads to a double-fracture:

- An internal disintegration – a shattered confidence and fearful vulnerability.
- An external disintegration – a withdrawal from society, and even (or perhaps especially) from those who are closest and most beloved.

In the grand scheme of things, my life has been sheltered and tame. I have not suffered terrible trauma or injury; I have not faced terminal illness or close family bereavement (yet). But as I wrote in *A Wilderness of Mirrors*, my depression has been triggered by several difficult experiences, as well as personality factors. This is not the place to unpack them all. Instead, it is better to focus on the few details that seem to resonate most with others.

In common with many, I endured several years of low-key bullying at my secondary school. There is no denying that I was privileged. In fact, I had the finest education money could buy (as we were frequently reminded), all the way from the ages of six to twenty-two. This easily puts me in the privileged 0.1%, globally speaking. Aside from the ethical and political dilemmas about private education, it would be churlish in the extreme not to be enormously grateful for what I was given.

The bullying was never physical, and always conducted with a shrewd, plausible deniability – the words 'but I was only joking' have had a grim resonance ever since. It constituted general mockery, the standard fare in any school, but it seemed at times to have a more malicious edge. The pain came from its constancy rather than its intensity. There might be days when even the major culprits could be pleasant and friendly, which was a welcome respite. But it never lasted long. This generated what I now recognize as a common problem. Psychologist Nick Duffell has written and broadcast extensively about what he describes, perhaps grandiosely, as 'boarding school survivor syndrome'.

One of my clients really hit the nail on the head. He said:
I became a strategic person, always on the lookout
for danger and how to turn every situation to my best

advantage. I still do it. It's exhausting. I don't know how
to stop doing it.

That was exactly it, I thought, it is a 'strategic survival
personality' that we are dealing with.[7]

That was certainly true of my situation. Furthermore, I never
mastered the art of handling it well. I never could triangulate
my responses to find the right mix of aloofness (in the hope
that they lost interest for failing to hit home, while risking the
implication that all was harmless), joviality (to show I could
take some self-deprecation and laugh with the best of them)
and participation (I dare say that, in darker moments, I joined
in when the target sights shifted away from me). But, on the
whole, I reacted in precisely the way I was expected to, which
no doubt all made 'good sport'.

Just one incident brings it home.

My secondary school was huge – more like a mini university, with 1,300 boys spread out across the town. All of us lived
in boarding houses of around fifty boys, some of which, for
historical reasons, had their own dining areas. The rest of us
ate our meals in a huge cafeteria complex, subdivided into
zones allotted to groups of three houses. As is the nature
of these things, our tables also tended to be unofficially
subdivided by year group. For some reason, I was late into
lunch one day, and so was last in our year to sit down. No
sooner had I put my tray down than the whole group, without
exception, stood up and moved en masse to another table. It
was utterly humiliating. It was obvious what had happened,
not only to everyone in my own house, but also to the other
boys in our zone. It required little coordination, and was
probably dreamt up only seconds before. They probably
thought nothing of it afterwards and had forgotten it a day or
two later. But it proved to be a formative moment for my own

sense of personal identity. There was evidently something about *me* that was unpalatable, awkward or essentially unacceptable. I didn't blame my schoolmates for what had happened. I blamed myself. I blamed who *I am*.

That is classic shame thinking. Because it happened in a place of explicit privilege, it produced what Duffell identifies as a double-bind. On one side, there is the shame for being shamefully treated (which 'must' have been deserved); on the other, the reality of the privileged context of these experiences makes the possibility of gaining sympathy or understanding seem remote. Many therefore suffer in silence. And thus, the infamous British stiff upper lip gets bred in yet another generation.

In a perverse mental feedback loop, this exacerbates the depression mindset. The more I sense the grounds for my shame, the worse the depression becomes. That, in turn, becomes yet another occasion for shame. For I now know that I am the *kind of person* who gets depression. I am not the strong, self-sufficient person who can stand on my own two feet. I am weak and fragile. I am less than I want to be; I am less than I should be. Or so it feels. No wonder they all moved when I sat down. Given the choice, I would have joined them.

**Freedom from shame?**

For the shamed person, forgiveness offers only partial respite . . . if any. Curt Thompson explains:

> Despite all we know about shame, containing it, let alone disposing of it, is a bit like grasping for mercury: the more pressure you use to seize it, the more evasive it becomes . . . It is ubiquitous, seeping into every nook and cranny of life. It is pernicious, infesting not just our thoughts but our

sensations, images, feelings and, of course, ultimately our behavior. It just doesn't seem to go away.[8]

The only hope is for the supposedly unlovable to find acceptance and welcome, to bask in the reassurance of knowing they are lovable and acceptable. Anything less is profoundly threatening and, perversely, compounds the shame. Note that it is more than being lov*ed* and accept*ed* in the past tense – that does not guarantee the future for the shamed person. Because there is always the anxiety, however deeply buried, that when others find out the 'real me', then they will eventually run a mile. For shame convinces me that I am unlov*able* and unaccept*able*.

To know the forgiveness of a specific misdeed is, of course, wonderful. That should never be underestimated. But that knowledge never alters the fact that I am *the kind of person* who does those misdeeds. I know that I *still* want to do them, even after trusting in their absolution. Paul the apostle understood that:

> I do not understand what I do. For what I want to do I do not do, but what I hate I do . . . For I do not do the good I want to do, but the evil I do not want to do – this I keep on doing . . . What a wretched man I am! Who will rescue me from this body that is subject to death?
> (Romans 7:15, 19, 24)

Shame can thus seem like the unavoidable consequence of honest self-appraisal. After all, who can honestly claim to have nothing to be ashamed of in life? Or to guarantee that there never will be? So, if this is such a universal challenge, the only real distinction between human beings is what we then do about our shame.

This brings real dangers for those in any sort of pastoral work. If my shame has caused such profound instability, then it is perhaps inevitable that we attempt to heal the wounds through cultivating the love and acceptance of the people we serve, if only to prevent future assaults. But not only is this flawed, since such acceptance can only be limited, it is also highly damaging. Our service of others can become a cover for our own self-service and, *in extremis*, generates what the psychologists call 'codependency'. I need others to be pastorally needy, in order for me to be able to meet those needs. Consequently, I have no real incentive for them to heal, but inadvertently sustain their dependence on me. Of course, this is the worst-case scenario. But I know I am not alone in being someone who has sought acceptance, as well as personal fulfilment, through the service of God and his people.

What balm then to discover an ancient prophet who antici-pated *precisely* the need! Isaiah here describes the promised divine blessing for the shamed:

> Instead of your shame
>   you will receive a double portion,
> and instead of disgrace
>   you will rejoice in your inheritance.
> And so you will inherit a double portion in your land,
>   and everlasting joy will be yours.
> (Isaiah 61:7)

Divine acceptance, like forgiveness, elicits joy. But, because of shame's ontological nature, the joy for such acceptance is bound to be more intense and settled, less shaken by life's confusions. Only God can truly heal the wounds of shame – other people can only go so far. This joy is 'everlasting', substantial and renewing. I love these words of Timothy Keller because they seem to me to capture the shock of it all perfectly:

> To be loved but not known is comforting but superficial. To be known and not loved is our greatest fear. But to be fully known and truly loved is, well, a lot like being loved by God. It is what we need more than anything. It liberates us from pretence, humbles us out of our self-righteousness, and fortifies us for any difficulty life can throw at us.[9]

In short, this is the wonder of Christian grace.

The diagram below seeks to draw these threads together, showing how the varied causes of shame lead to the common fear of exposure, which, in turn, leads to either withdrawal or its polar opposite, a pre-emptive self-exposure or flaunting. Grace brings the intervention that is uniquely able to break these destructive mental loops. But notice that the focus of grace when dealing with guilt is different from what is needed for shame. It is simply not enough for the shamed

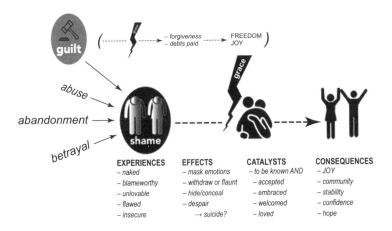

| EXPERIENCES | EFFECTS | CATALYSTS | CONSEQUENCES |
|---|---|---|---|
| – naked | – mask emotions | – to be known AND | – JOY |
| – blameworthy | – withdraw or flaunt | – accepted | – community |
| – unlovable | – hide/conceal | – embraced | – stability |
| – flawed | – despair | – welcomed | – confidence |
| – insecure | → suicide? | – loved | – hope |

person to be told of forgiveness. A different, parallel, pastoral response is needed, which is why it is placed on a separate line.

### The catalyst of grace

Grace is an intervention, a breaking in of what is good, affirmative and wholesome, despite what we deserve or expect. In fact, that doesn't quite capture it. If it was deserved, it couldn't be called grace. For grace is the antithesis of karma. It is the only thing that can break the rigidity of a universe created with cause and effect ingrained. Perhaps that's why grace can only originate from God, because only he can break the laws he has made. Only a Creator can perform miracles.

God's grace in Christ brings forgiveness, of course. His death on the cross achieved an astonishing victory: 'In him we have redemption through his blood, the forgiveness of sins, in accordance with the riches of God's grace that he lavished on us' (Ephesians 1:7–8).

As the diagram on the previous page illustrates, it is the catalyst that destroys guilt's prison cell, as Charles Wesley so wonderfully described:

> Long my imprisoned spirit lay
> Fast bound in sin and nature's night;
> Thine eye diffused a quickening ray,
> I woke, the dungeon flamed with light;
> My chains fell off, my heart was free,
> I rose, went forth, and followed Thee.[10]

But, as already noted, it is not enough to have past sins dealt with. What about a broken nature that repeatedly finds itself falling, perhaps even with a repeated sense of being imprisoned? Will the well of forgiveness ever run dry?

I heard recently from someone who went to work with Jackie Pullinger. She has been ministering to the drug addicts and prostitutes of Hong Kong since 1966, focusing on the old slums of Kowloon Walled City (until that was demolished in 1993). The speaker described one addict whose life was revolutionized by the ministry. He finally managed to come off heroin . . . on his *eighteenth* attempt. She asked the simple question – how many government programmes, or any other charitable or church programmes for that matter, would exhibit such patience? Even the most kind-hearted would struggle to avoid cynicism on the sixteenth or seventeenth attempt. But this man now runs his own business, employing many ex-addicts, and has been clean for years.

This is the counter-intuitive, other-worldly nature of grace. It keeps holding out hope, when all else have lost it. John Forrester wonderfully summarizes it like this:

> Grace for guilt is unmerited forgiveness. Grace for shame is unmerited acceptance. (And grace for anxiety is unmerited security.) . . . As Patton rightly observes, 'Guilt can be more nearly dealt with according to rational principle, whereas shame is inevitably relational and personal.'[11]

Acceptance – that's the key for the shamed. Without equivocation or qualification. To generalize slightly, forgiveness is primarily about the past, whereas acceptance is all about the future, come what may. Of course, the future is unknown, but the intervention of grace-filled acceptance is the catalyst that changes everything, that enables a person crippled by shame to start facing the future with hope. To help grasp this, we must consider what it means to come face to face with God himself.

## Face to face with God

One of the most beautiful prayers of the Old Testament is the so-called Aaronic or priestly blessing. God himself revealed it to Moses to pass on to his brother:

> The LORD bless you
>     and keep you;
> the LORD make his face shine on you
>     and be gracious to you;
> the LORD turn his face towards you
>     and give you peace.
> (Numbers 6:24–26)

What often gets missed is the implausibility of this blessing. I don't mean that God fails to bless, or that he cannot be relied upon to be gracious or grant peace. It is simply the fact that having his face shine on a person is risky. Moses knew this from personal experience.

It was a paradox. The apparent contradiction is bluntly stated within the space of only a few paragraphs. Moses' unique privilege is clear – and is described in remarkable terms: 'The LORD would speak to Moses face to face, as a man speaks with his friend' (Exodus 33:11).

This was his experience at Mount Sinai's summit, while God fleshed out the old covenant with Abraham by revealing the full extent of the law.

But we find these words from God on the very same page. Moses has asked to see God's glory (which is his essence, his *god*ness, literally his 'weightiness'), and the response is a partial assent: he will be able to see God's goodness as he passes, but Moses must hide in a cleft in the rocks for protection. The reason is clear: '. . . you cannot see my face, for no one may see me and live' (Exodus 33:20). It doesn't make sense. One moment there is extraordinary intimacy, the next, restraint and exclusion.

But Bible writers do tend to know what they are doing – and apparent contradictions, especially at such close quarters, must be provocatively deliberate. Exodus 33 dramatizes the dilemma at the heart of the old covenant – namely that God's desire for intimacy with his people is thwarted by their disqualifying, and indeed endangering, sinfulness. The entire sacrificial system in the tabernacle, revealed in Exodus and given detail in Leviticus, is God's response to the dilemma. But it seems to speak more of exclusion than access. So, at the climax of Exodus, when God's glory finally comes down into the Israelite camp, there were restrictions: 'Moses could not enter the tent of meeting because the cloud had settled on it, and the glory of the LORD filled the tabernacle' (Exodus 40:35).

This dilemma never finds any resolution in the pages of the Old Testament. No-one, not even Moses, sees the face of Yahweh. So does this render the Aaronic blessing mere wishful thinking, or even a cruel joke? It would seem so . . . until we reach the New Testament era.

### Face to face with Jesus

John's momentous words in the prologue to his Gospel now have far greater resonance:

> The Word became flesh and made his dwelling among us.
> We have seen his glory, the glory of the One and only Son,
> who came from the Father, full of grace and truth . . .
> No one has ever seen God, but the one and only Son, who
> is himself God and is in the closest relationship with the
> Father, has made him known.
> (John 1:14, 18)

How is the old covenant dilemma resolved? By Jesus – who is God himself, living amongst us, despite our sin and shame. And John knew it first-hand – he could honestly say that he had seen God's glory with his own eyes! Jesus made visible the invisible God. 'We have seen his glory!' What's more, no-one had to hide in a rock to see it. How was this possible? Well, in John's telling, Jesus' place of glory is the most unlikely place of all: at the crucifixion. Here he explains it himself:

> The hour has come for the Son of Man to be glorified. Very truly I tell you, unless a grain of wheat falls to the ground and dies, it remains only a single seed. But if it dies, it produces many seeds.
> (John 12:23)

In essence, he teaches that he must die so that others might live. The cross is where we truly see the weightiness of God.

But what has this to do with the shamed person? Everything. Because the cross establishes once and for all God's attitude to those who come to him: extravagant love. Even when we fail. Perhaps especially when we fail. For Jesus knows us better than we know ourselves. We can't surprise him; we can't shock him; we can't go too low for him. He died for us. No shame is too great.

As every minister knows, this seems too good to be true – and too dangerous to proclaim. Because it seems to be a 'get-out-of-jail-free' card, with no strings attached. It promises forgiveness for all past wrongdoing, and full acceptance for the future. As if it didn't matter how we responded or lived. Which is, of course, nonsense. But we have only begun to understand the scandal of grace if we find ourselves asking the question Paul posed in Romans 6: 'What shall we say, then? Shall we go on sinning, so that grace may increase? By no means! We are those who have died to sin; how can we live in it any longer?' (Romans 6:1–2). A useful thought experiment will diagnose how well we have grasped this.

In the final hours of Jesus' life, he is dragged from trial to trial. Some of his closest friends try to keep up with him in support, but just as when their good intentions to keep him company in the Garden of Gethsemane failed, so they find it is too dangerous. Peter gets further than most though. He seems to have forgotten the prediction, only a few hours before, that he would publicly disown Jesus 'before the cock crows' (Luke 22:34).

He is in the heart of enemy territory, though. Standing around the warming fire in the high priest's courtyard, Peter is asked by three separate people if he was acquainted with the man under arrest. Three times he claims he is not, with what seems like growing desperation. But then, just as the cock crows, Luke includes a detail overlooked by the other Gospel writers: 'The Lord turned and looked straight at Peter. Then Peter remembered the word the Lord had spoken to him' (Luke 22:61).

Peter and Jesus – face to face, albeit in highly stressful circumstances. Presumably, Jesus was being escorted out by the guards at that precise moment, or could see the courtyard from inside the house. Face to face. Here's the thought experiment: what was the expression on Jesus' face as he looked at Peter?

- Anger?
- Disappointment?
- Despair?

It is speculative, of course – but I am confident that it was none of these. It goes back to why Jesus predicted Peter's failure in the first place. His reasons are clear: 'Simon, Simon, Satan has asked to sift all of you as wheat. But I have prayed for you, Simon, that your faith may not fail. And when you have turned back, strengthen your brothers' (Luke 22:31–32).

Jesus knew what would happen; more to the point, he knew exactly what Peter was like. And yet he *still* had a job for him. So what was the expression on Jesus' face? Love. It had to be. Love and acceptance.

No wonder Peter ran out sobbing. The agony and the shame of it. To begin with, that face of love made it so much worse. But I have no doubt that he remembered it for the rest of his life – especially when he slipped up or failed. A love that knows us and our nature – and is still interested. He perseveres with us. Such is the overwhelming wonder of God's grace, the only true catalyst for change for the shamed. This explains why these words in the letter to the Hebrews are now some of my most treasured: 'Both the one who makes people holy and those who are made holy are of the same family. So Jesus is not ashamed to call them brothers and sisters' (Hebrews 2:11).

Jesus is not ashamed to know me, even me! It is incredible. It seems too good to be true. But no, it is so good precisely because it is true.

So, because of Jesus, we can truly claim the full treasure of that great Aaronic blessing. His face can, and will, truly shine on us. And it is a face with the look of sacrificial love.

The problem is that such extravagant kindness and generosity tend to be in short supply in society and, sadly, even in the church. We are much more likely to hear of people experiencing something closer to the psalmist's pain:

I live in disgrace all day long,
    and my face is covered with shame
at the taunts of those who reproach and revile me,
    because of the enemy, who is bent on revenge.
(Psalm 44:15–16)

It is especially hard when others take it upon themselves to 'heap coals of fire' on the shamed, even with the best of pastoral motives, when they don't seem to have faced up to their sin. There may be a time and place for such an approach, for the most recalcitrant and rebellious. But it is highly unlikely to be the case for the person battling the black dog. In fact, it may well have the most devastating effect, merely serving to propel a shamed person towards the ultimate sanction of concealment: the subject of the next chapter.

## 6. THE CLOSING

This is a chapter I dreaded writing, one I never wanted to write, and one I've hated writing. But it needs to be written because the subject won't go away.

I should start by making explicit what is self-evident. I am still here. I have not done anything alarming. Thoughts have never yet become deeds. Every time the darkest thoughts eclipse my mental horizon, I do somehow come to my senses for one reason and one reason only. My family. I could not do anything to myself that would devastate my parents, brother, wife and children. I understand enough of these things to know that survivors rarely come close to getting over it. So, if there is one thing to stop me in my tracks, it is the potential grief of those closest to me. I never want deliberately to deprive my parents of a son, my wife of a husband, my children of a father, my good friends of a good friend. It's as simple as that. That is why I persevere.

Except it isn't as simple as that, is it?

Sometimes (often?), the awareness of an action's consequences is an insufficient deterrent to pursuing an action's course. Life is full of that. If it were not, there would be no need of hospitals, law courts or even the Christian gospel. And if anything can be said for certain about thoughts of ending one's own life, then it is the fact that it is rarely simple. For, unfortunately, I do understand those who have gone through with committing suicide (there, I've used the word at last).

So I know how profoundly unhelpful some of the pastoral approaches of the well-meaning can be. I have read various pieces produced by well-intentioned, and indeed professional, counselling centres, designed to help friends to understand those with suicidal feelings. They usually do a good job. However, they are not always ideal for someone in the throes of the darkest thoughts. For example, one included two or three paragraphs on the selfishness of suicide. A friend who was given it at a crisis point found it overwhelming. It merely served to ratchet up the guilt she already felt – with potentially devastating consequences.

Those who contemplate the ultimate course have historically been charged with all kinds of failings and character flaws: cowardice . . . lack of backbone . . . selfishness . . . weakness . . . even sinful arrogance. Of course, there may well be shreds of truth in any, if not all, of them. But even after putting the ad hominem attacks to one side, there are many important arguments to make against it, from the pastoral through to the philosophical and theological. It is hard to conceive of circumstances in which suicide might be unreservedly positive. It is no accident that in English we use the phrase 'take one's own life'. For we're taking it from others – loved ones, acquaintances and colleagues, strangers even to whom we might have been a blessing. And, ultimately, we're taking it from the Creator of life himself.

Down the centuries, thinkers have considered the problem, and there has been near unanimity in opposition to suicide.

So, in the thirteenth century, Thomas Aquinas's case was very influential. Consequently, in medieval England, suicides were denied Christian burial in consecrated ground, and a suicide's assets were subject to confiscation by the state (as punishment for the 'theft' of the potential feudal service owed to the king). If a jury declared that a death was caused by suicide, the perpetrator would be given a so-called 'profane' burial at a crossroads (to confuse his or her ghost!) and a stake through the heart (to prevent the ghost from escaping!), a practice that only ceased in the early nineteenth century. Then, right up until 1871, it was still legal for the British taxman to seize a suicide's assets, and, even more astonishingly, taking one's own life was still legally a criminal act as late as 1960. This bizarre convergence of deep theologizing, folk religion and crude superstition has thankfully been swept away here (although that is not always the case even in other parts of Europe).

There is much greater sympathy for the problem today than there has been for centuries, if ever. That is not enough to prevent fears and awkwardness surrounding it, however. No wonder it is rarely talked about. Then again, I can barely talk about it. So, it's not surprising.

Such reticence is rarely helpful. Talking about it has repeatedly been proven to reduce the likelihood by a significant margin of going through with suicidal feelings. Far from putting ideas into someone's head (which is the classic fear that friends have in raising the subject), it can come as a relief (if sensitively done). Even the most determined have ambivalent feelings about their intentions – a listening friend can literally be a lifesaver.

So, having explained why I won't – to ease loved ones' feelings more than anything – and a little of why the subject is honoured mainly by its avoidance, we should now consider why anyone might want to. This feels like sacred ground in a way, or, at least, like thin ice. Some of what follows has never passed my lips. The only one who truly knows is the Lord himself – but that is a point that has sometimes confused more than consoled me (as will become clear). For some reason, I have always found it easier to express myself on paper. So, if we meet in person, please don't expect me necessarily to be able to expand on what I write now. I do it in part to help me find the words for myself, and in part to help those who can't imagine the words.

I have loved this poem by Yeats for years, mainly for its last couplet. It is simple, almost clichéd:

> Had I the heavens' embroidered cloths,
> Enwrought with golden and silver light,
> The blue and the dim and the dark cloths
> Of night and light and the half-light;
> I would spread the cloths under your feet:
> But I, being poor, have only my dreams;
> I have spread my dreams under your feet;
> Tread softly because you tread on my dreams.[1]

In the context of this chapter, however, we might give it a final twist.

> Tread gingerly since you tread on my nightmares.

## Precedents in pain

My first awareness of the issue came in a very weird way. The husband of one of my grandmother's cousins took his own life when I was a teenager in the 1980s. I think I must have met him perhaps once or twice, but I don't recall much more about him. I never heard any details – if it was discussed in the family (and it must have been), it would only have been done in hushed tones and far away from youthful ears.

I would find myself thinking about him quite a lot, however. He apparently prided himself on wearing very good clothes . . . and several of his office shirts were passed on to me. They were beautifully made, very comfortable, and lasted me for years. But every time I put one on, his laundry label in the collar caught my eye, and I would think about him. I found it impossible to imagine how matters could have got so dark for him that he felt there was no alternative.

It never occurred to me, of course, that I might discover for myself.

Statistics suggest that we should all expect to encounter mental illness in some form or another – either in ourselves, or in loved ones. Who knows how accurate this is, but the commonly bandied figure for those who will experience some form of depression during their lives is 25%. It doesn't especially matter – all that should concern us is that the number is BIG! Then, of that number, a proportion will inevitably have suicidal thoughts. Following through with those thoughts is thankfully rare – as the International Association for Suicide Prevention says, 'Suicide is complex. It usually occurs gradually, progressing from suicidal thoughts, to planning, to attempting suicide and finally dying by suicide.'[2]

This is what happened for over 6,100 British people in 2014 (that is 10.8 per 100,000). Most alarmingly, the highest rate in this country (at 26.5 per 100,000) is found amongst men aged 45–49.[3] That's my demographic! So here I am, sitting squarely, as I write, in the primary risk category.

But I can already hear some saying, 'But shouldn't it be different for you? You're a Christian. You're a church minister. You have a great family and a job. You're supposed to be the sorted one, with the answers to help those of us without them. You shouldn't have problems like this. Perhaps you're in the wrong job!' And so on, ad infinitum.

I don't think I am in the wrong job. But neither can I deny the reality of these thoughts. So what should I do? Can any sense be made of it?

## Ancient precedents

The Bible contains accounts of a number of individuals who took their own life. But the list, it must be said, is hardly inspiring:

- Abimelek (Judges 9:52–54)
- Samson (Judges 16:25–30)
- King Saul (1 Samuel 31:4)
- Saul's armour bearer (1 Samuel 31:5)
- Ahithophel (2 Samuel 17:23)
- Zimri (1 Kings 16:15–20)
- Judas Iscariot (Matthew 27:3–5)

None of them are individuals with whom we might naturally sympathize, let alone admire (with the possible exception of Saul's armour bearer).

### A psalmist at his wits' end

But several Bible heroes did face the darkest thoughts, of whom David has already been considered. We do not find him articulating them explicitly, but he gets as close as it's possible to get:

My heart pounds, my strength fails me;
even the light has gone from my eyes . . .

> For I am about to fall,
>     and my pain is ever with me.
>    (Psalm 38:10, 17)

It's as if he is edging, exhausted and depleted, towards a precipice, feeling overwhelmed by the vertiginous inevitability of falling. He can't take it any more.

Or take Psalm 55:

> My heart is in anguish within me;
>     the terrors of death have fallen on me.
> Fear and trembling have beset me;
>     horror has overwhelmed me.
> I said, 'Oh, that I had the wings of a dove!
>     I would fly away and be at rest.
> I would flee far away
>     and stay in the desert;
> I would hurry to my place of shelter,
>     far from the tempest and storm.'
>    (Psalm 55:4–8)

What is a suicidal thought if not, ultimately, the longing for escape? Pains and fears seem too bleak, the trials too overpowering. It makes little difference if they are problems of my own making, or circumstances entirely beyond my control. Facing them seems futile and pointless. The only thing one can think of is for it all to stop: for the internal clamour of the brain blizzard to be silenced, for the bludgeoning feelings of self-loathing to be restrained. Well, you would . . . wouldn't *you*?

Barring the swooping down of the Great Eagles summoned by Gandalf to rescue Bilbo and Sam from Mount Doom,[4] most of us need to find our own solutions. And suicide is certainly one. Or so it seems.

### A prosperous man who lost it all

Job was nothing if not straight-talking. That was just as well, since his friends were hardly reticent. He responds to Bildad's first speech in no uncertain terms:

> I loathe my very life;
>> therefore I will give free rein to my complaint
>> and speak out in the bitterness of my soul.
> I say to God: do not declare me guilty,
>> but tell me what charges you have against me.
> Does it please you to oppress me,
>> to spurn the work of your hands,
>> while you smile on the plans of the wicked?
> (Job 10:1–3)

This is not petulant angst – he truly had lost everything: his vast wealth (as indicated by the thousands of livestock and the many staff who worked for him) was lost in various attacks by foreign raiding parties. That was hard enough to bear. But every single one of his children died when a hurricane destroyed the house they were partying in, leaving only their grieving parents. Finally, to add insult to injury, he loses his physical health, and his wife starts taunting him for his stubborn trust in God's sovereign goodness. He is as alone as it is possible to be.

If ever there was a situation that would result in post-traumatic stress disorder, then this was it. Job's psychological affliction then was a direct consequence of his circumstances. His response here, therefore, is no surprise. Everything in life that brought blessings or joy to him had gone. So what was there to live for? 'I loathe my very life.' There's no trace of cowardice or selfishness there. It is a cry of agony and despair.

## A prophet at the end of his tether

Perhaps the best-known biblical example of suicidal thoughts that never get implemented is Elijah. After his bruising and shattering contest with Jezebel's prophets of Baal on Mount Carmel, he must run for his life. He collapses in exhaustion in the desert and prays, 'I have had enough, LORD . . . Take my life; I am no better than my ancestors' (1 Kings 19:4). You will not find this prayer in church liturgies from any culture, as far as I can tell. But it was prayed by one of the great saints of old.

I have heard this passage preached to illustrate the Lord's perfect pastoral sensitivity to an exhausted, but faithful, servant. And it is certainly that. Elijah endured sustained and extreme stress over a considerable period. It is no surprise he was traumatized and broken by it. His is a classic case of ministry burn-out. The way he is cared for in the subsequent verses is telling:

- He is allowed to fall asleep (19:5).
- An angel wakes him to give him food (19:5).
- After having his fill, he sleeps again (19:6).
  Then he is given more food (19:7).

Then he travels for forty days and nights (as if echoing Israel's forty years in the wilderness and anticipating Jesus' forty days). After Elijah's journey, preachers often then home in on the fact that he is encouraged to listen out for God at Horeb (that is, Mount Sinai): but he doesn't hear him in the hurricane or earthquake or fire. Instead, he hears him in a low whisper (19:11–13). We are, therefore, privileged to eavesdrop on a moment of exquisite gentleness and divine care.

This is certainly a reasonable, truthful and helpful explanation. It fits perfectly with the way that God works with the broken. Isaiah revealed this aspect of God's character with the beautifully tender words:

> A bruised reed he will not break,
>     and a smouldering wick he will not snuff out.[5]
> (Isaiah 42:3)

Then, of course, we see it in Jesus himself throughout the Gospels.

But there is quite possibly something even more subtle going on here. We are told that God twice asked Elijah what he was doing there (1 Kings 19:9, 13). Yet the Lord has clearly brought him – that's why the angel made sure he was well fed. The question hardly seems prompted by divine ignorance. Rather, it was a divine teaching moment for the prophet. Here he was at Sinai, at *the* cave (as opposed to any old cave), because, as we saw in the previous chapter, this was where Moses experienced the passing of God's glory. Elijah will have that too.

Even more significantly, this was where God gave of the Law through Moses. This was the location of God's greatest revelation in the Jewish Scriptures. In fact, a perfectly plausible translation of 19:12 is: 'after the fire the sound of a thin silence'.[6] To put it another way, after the tempestuous display of natural forces, there was . . . nothing apart from the atmosphere, the sound of silence. Why? Because God has already spoken. There is nothing to add to his word.

This does *not* mean that Elijah is a failure. It is simply that he has lost his grip on reality. Nothing has changed the foundation of the covenant. But his exhaustion and fear have robbed him of that security. If he is not actually depressed, he certainly displays many of the symptoms. He is clearly burned out. So God graciously brings him to this point to remind and restore him.

He needs sleep and food and . . . a renewed vision of God who has never left him, one who has already said everything that needed to be said.

It is on this basis that suicidal thoughts need to be met with gentle care, sleep and food (both physical and spiritual). Someone who has been 'running on empty' for too long needs refilling at every level. This is practical wisdom. And balanced diets, sleep and work patterns are usually the first things to consider when there are problems with mental health. Modern culture has unfortunately compartmentalized life to such an extent that we forget how integrated we all are. As Sarah Sylstra writes,

> In the days of the Reformation or the later Puritans, a pastor would be consulted for any malady and be somewhat knowledgeable about all areas. Today, a physician treats the body, a psychologist treats the mind, and a pastor treats the spirit. But that separation can lead to trouble, since the spiritual, emotional, and physical affect each other.[7]

I am *by no means* suggesting that pastors should resume such a comprehensive role, any more than barbers should take up dentistry just because their medieval forebears did. This is especially important where mental illness is concerned. There are complexities and nuances for which only basic pastoral training can never equip us. So we should be very wary when ministers presume to give medical advice in contradiction to professionals, particularly if it entails unilaterally coming off medication. That is folly, and potentially harmful.

The dreadful reality is that each person's affliction is so isolatingly different, and few can be treated straightforwardly. For some, it goes on for a few weeks; for others, it endures for years. For some, medication is a lifesaver; for others, it is irrelevant or even detrimental. For some, there is an acute spiritual problem at its heart; for others, there really isn't. The key point from Sylstra's insight is the wisdom in taking a holistic approach. We should avoid the compartmentalization to which moderns are so prone. Everything needs to be factored in, from diet and exercise to lifestyle and work patterns.

## Disoriented in darkness

Apparently, the latest fad amongst Californian health fanatics and experience junkies is the sensory deprivation tank. The idea is to lie in room-temperature water inside an enclosed, darkened space for an extended period and see what happens. One writer was stunned by it:

> I slid feet first and lay face-up in the warm water, and, sure enough, misjudged myself, routes, locations, perceptions, and level of control.
>
> I cannot stress how quickly the following happened. Immediately after I lay on my back and with my arms at my sides, my brain went haywire.
>
> Yes, on paper, I was merely floating in a tank wearing earplugs. I won't pretend to know the science behind why I lost control, but it was mental chaos. It started with the instant feeling of reclining in a hospital bed hurling through outer space. But I hadn't moved at all.
>
> Meanwhile, I was wrestling a legitimate panic attack. My heart pounded. My mind was an indecipherable jumble of fear. It was a terrifying feeling for which I had no context to compare. It felt like I was going to die if I didn't get out of that tank.[8]

He was then able to calm himself down, and relaxed for the rest of his ninety-minute session. But I was struck by his description. He is clearly describing a panic attack, which is not the same as depression, of course. But the effect of this attack closely resembles my experience of depression's brain blizzard, differing only in its limited duration. I think this helps to explain why suicidal thoughts can begin to take a grip. One gets fixated on escape.

Kathryn Greene-McCreight puts it well:

> Tasks, busyness, gardening, tidying up: distractions. Mustn't think, mustn't be conscious, mustn't reflect. This escape from consciousness is at the heart of suicidal energy. It is *not* wanting to hurt the self. It is simply wanting *not to hurt*. When I am depressed, it seems that the only way not to hurt is to cease being a center of consciousness.[9]

You see, we know all too well what we are missing, but simply cannot see how to get it back.

This is especially true for the Christian with depression, I suspect. It explains why someone who has convictions about God, in particular his purposes and providence, can lose the plot so dramatically. More to the point, it explains how a Christian minister (who is employed to convince others of this stuff, for goodness sake!) can find himself so overwhelmed that the ultimate escape seems the *only* escape. I think that this is what makes it peculiarly difficult for 'professional' Christians. Depression robs us of confidence in the very salve we are commissioned and employed to offer others.

### Loss of perception

Depression's sensory deprivation is insidious – it displaces the reality of the objective world with a phantasm, a plausible alternative that is darker, more nightmarish. It robs one of all positivity. Compliments get filtered out, intentions interpreted as masked ignorance or malice, the future becomes doom-laden and menacing. The ability to reason clearly, which is a challenge to many of us at the best of times, evaporates completely.

### Loss of perspective

The upshot is that the classic conundrum of theodicy – the problem of how God can be just, good and sovereign in the face of rampant suffering and evil – becomes all too personal. How can God be what he claims to be? Even more disturbingly, how can I know he genuinely exists and is at work in the world? Is he not, in truth, that archetypal psychological crutch, but one that proves as reliable as a mirage of an oasis in a desert? My entire career path (such as it is) depends on the fact that he does exist – and so does my worldview. So to have that called into question at the most existential level is profoundly disorientating.

The Christian knows that we are limited and finite in every way – it is in the very nature of being human. But we claim to know the one who sees and hears everything. He is the 'Ancient of Days', who sits on heaven's throne, sovereign over the cosmos. He reveals truth to us from his unique point of view. In other words, he sits at the summit, but relays aspects of his view to those of us in the valleys and foothills. He gives us glimpses of the big picture (or at least as much as we can bear or comprehend).

To lose a sense of him is thus to lose all perspective.

However, we should take this further. From within the sensory deprivation tank, the experience is akin to the central challenge of postmodernism: how do I know what I know about anything? This is a question that has perplexed me for the last twenty-five years intellectually and culturally. But it has been most alarming to find myself similarly adrift psychologically as well.

It is not surprising then that a third loss follows.

### Loss of purpose

I can't perceive what is real. I have no overarching perspective from which to discern reality. Consequently, I cannot see the point. I am besieged by hostility and certain disaster.

So what would seem to you the wisest course of action in such circumstances? How would you drag yourself up and keep motivated? None of the consolations of grace that we considered in the previous chapters – the wonders of forgiveness for guilt and acceptance for shame – registers or seems real. God seems absent, and so there is nothing left.

- 'Oh, that I had the wings of a dove! I would fly away and be at rest,' sang David.
- 'I loathe my very life; therefore I will give free rein to my complaint,' cried Job.
- 'I have had enough, LORD. Take my life,' prayed Elijah.

It really *does* seem the case that darkness is my closest friend.

Except I have family and loved ones. I can see that even in the storm. I can't necessarily feel their importance, but I do know it. I see that I mean much to them. I know enough of what it would do to them if I carried this darkness through. There would never be any return from that. I hate to be the cause of pain.

But it doesn't stop the thoughts. It is, sadly, the case that in the last twelve or more years, not a week has gone by without the thought of it. That is, I believe, because of what one could call depression fatigue. I'm just so exhausted by the energy required to keep afloat, to preserve a brave face, to control the churn of volcanic lava. So I yearn for only one thing: rest. Permanent rest.

I'd only known of David's heartfelt longing for dove's wings through singing (as a rather bad treble) Mendelssohn's rather sentimental and effete setting of Psalm 55. I love much of the composer's work, but to my ears, this version completely lacks the urgent desperation of David's plea. I suppose that this is one reason why I failed to take the psalm as seriously as I ought to have done. But, on revisiting it more recently, I found it resonated profoundly. To fly away and be at rest – yes, that's *exactly* it.

I wouldn't plan in the way that some do – possibly because I'm not the obsessive organizer type – only idle thoughts of that rest from the churn and confusion. Too many pills? Linger on a busy London street and then a little 'slip' in front of a bus? Or a tube train? So easy. So straightforward.

Except, of course, it's not. One dear friend did throw himself in front of a London Underground train, and I visited him in hospital the next day. I've never seen so many tubes and bandages. Parts of his body had been reduced to indefinable pulp. But he survived and made a remarkable recovery – or rather, he recovered physically, at least. But even these kinds of intentions have a habit of going awry. And it really isn't fair on the poor traumatized driver, let alone everybody else.

Then the mental loops crank up.

'I can't believe you're thinking like this. Just stop it. Just stop. But I want it to stop . . . please stop . . .'

'Oh, Lord, is there no end to this . . . please Lord. . . are you there? . . . have you noticed? Nobody else understands . . . do you? LORD!'

'Wake up, dead man ... I'm alone in this world. And a f***ed-up world it is too ... Tell me the story ... about eternity ...,' as Bono sings.[10]

How was it that I believed in the 'story about eternity' in the first place? Was it just a delusion? Is everything just a delusion?

And so the cycle goes. I never said it made much logical sense. But I'm so bored of it. A cracked record.

And someone who is wrung out and exhausted seeks just one thing – sleep.

## Gentleness not threats

To find someone who understands this from first-hand experience is rare but precious. It was a surprise, therefore, suddenly to realize that the apostle Paul did. He was someone who suffered immensely: insults and scorn; strenuous physical labour and long journeys on foot; extreme poverty and future uncertainty; beatings, floggings and stoning; court appearances and imprisonments, shipwrecks and sickness. Having been hooked on some of the better forensics TV series, I sometimes wonder what a pathologist would conclude from a post-mortem on his body. The scars, bone fractures and general wear and tear would have been astonishing, testimony to a very tough life.

So there is no surprise in these famous words from one of his last letters, written from a Roman prison: 'For to me, to live is Christ and to die is gain' (Philippians 1:21).

That is an understatement. He knows that death is not ultimately an end, but a beginning. But he also knows that it brings an end to a life of pain and suffering that he knew first-hand, in order to begin a life of sinless rest, bliss and joy. No wonder it is 'gain'!

But how he continues is truly startling:

> If I am to go on living in the body, this will mean fruitful
> labour for me. Yet what shall I choose? I do not know! I am
> torn between the two: I desire to depart and be with Christ,
> which is better by far; but it is more necessary for you that
> I remain in the body. Convinced of this, I know that I will
> remain, and I will continue with all of you for your progress
> and joy in the faith, so that through my being with you again
> your boasting in Christ Jesus will abound on account of me.
> (Philippians 1:22–26)

He has a strategic ministry on earth – that much is clear. He
has plenty of reasons to continue: there are many people he
loves, and they love him (witness the Ephesians' tearful
farewells at the Miletus docks in Acts 20:37–38).

What is astonishing is his difficulty in choosing between
staying or going! To go and be with Christ is 'better by far'!
That is his deepest desire. It's no contest. But the matter is
clearly settled in his mind by the fact that there is still work
for him to do. It is simply a matter of timing. It is comforting,
nevertheless, to find that the apostle can be open about
wanting to depart. He is at least sympathetic to the tug.

My challenge is how I get from the longing to depart for
rest and restoration that is so overwhelming that it eclipses
everything else, to a healthy acceptance, and even relishing,
of life's tensions. For the Christian life has always been a
tension between the 'now' and the 'not yet' – between what
God promises us in this life, and what we expect in our life
after life.

This is the challenge that shapes the rest of the book.

INTERLUDE

Before moving on, I want to include a song that somehow manages to draw all the book's threads so far together. Andrew Peterson is a songwriter whom I have come to appreciate greatly in recent years.

Here he captures brilliantly the pain of living in tension between the despair of mental illness and clinging to hopeful faith. Because my work means I travel a lot, this song somehow manages to evoke my whole story.

**The Rain Keeps Falling**

I tried to be brave but I hid in the dark
I sat in that cave and I prayed for a spark
To light up all the pain that remained in my heart
And the rain kept falling

Down on the roof of the church where I cried
I could hear all the laughter and love and I tried
To get up and get out but a part of me died
And the rain kept falling down

Well I'm scared if I open myself to be known
I'll be seen and despised and be left all alone
So I'm stuck in this tomb and you won't move the stone
And the rain keeps falling

Somewhere the sun is a light in the sky
But I'm dying in North Carolina and I
Can't believe there's an end to this season of night
And the rain keeps falling down
Falling down

There's a woman at home and she's praying for a light
My children are there and they love me in spite
Of the shadow I know that they see in my eyes
And the rain keeps falling

I'm so tired of this game, of these songs, of the rote
I'm already ashamed of the line I just wrote
But it's true and it feels like I can't sing a note
And the rain keeps falling down
Falling down, Falling down
    *Peace, be still, Peace, be still*

My daughter and I put the seeds in the dirt
And every day now we've been watching the earth
For a sign that this death will give way to a birth
And the rain keeps falling

Down on the soil where the sorrow is laid
And the secret of life is igniting the grave
And I'm dying to live but I'm learning to wait
And the rain is falling
    *Peace, be still, Peace, be still*

*(Peace, be still)*
I just want to be new again
   *(Peace, be still)*
I just want to be closer to You again
   *(Peace, be still)*
Lord, I can't find the song
I'm so tired and I'm always so wrong
   *(Peace, be still)*
Help me be brave tonight
Jesus, please help me out of this cave tonight
   *(Peace, be still)*
I've been calling and calling
This rain just keeps falling
   *(Peace, be still)*
I've been calling and calling
But this rain just keeps falling and falling
   *(Peace, be still)*
Is it You? Is it You?
   *(Peace, be still)*
Is it true? Is it You?
   *(Peace, peace)*[1]

PART 2:

VENTURING TOWARDS THE LIGHT

## 7. THE WAY

As it happens, I embark on this chapter having just returned from speaking at a couple of small conferences for pastors. These are run specifically to give ministers who pour themselves out for others the space and freedom to receive and be refreshed. Being there was a great encouragement for both Rachel and me, despite technically being on duty!

The organizers had programmed an interview time in which they wanted me to talk about my mental health challenges, and I was happy to do this. A friend of Rachel's later made a striking comment. She remarked on the relief of hearing from someone in the midst of, rather than having won, a personal battle. It is obviously encouraging to hear testimonies of people who have survived terrible challenges or illness and come out stronger or restored. That gives hope to others with similar trials. But it is not so helpful if our 'testimony diet' is exclusively a string of victories and miraculous interventions. For, then, those enduring chronic pain or difficulty will invariably feel worse. They need help for those times when there is *no* change. How does one persevere *then*?

The truth is, I have no idea how long this susceptibility to brain blizzards, increased heart rates and dark clouds will last. I have no clue whether I will need medication for only a few more months or for the rest of my life. In short, I don't know the future. It's obvious, really. Despite the absurd claim of the idiom, the future is *not* foreseeable!

The question is how we persevere in the face of such uncertainty. How do we learn to take each day as it comes? The starting point must surely be our expectations. What do we really expect in life?

## Managing our expectations

King David could truly be said to have lived a roller-coaster life. He endured a string of startling promotions and reversals – each must have been a shock to his system. This continued even after he had spent years on the Jewish throne. One pertinent example from the early days is Psalm 34, written at a particularly stressful time. Its subtitle informs us that he was on the run from King Saul's homicidal rages and 'pretended to be insane before Abimelek'.[1] After this deliverance, David was full of praise and gratitude to God, in the course of which he wrote one of the most tender and comforting lines in Scripture:

> The LORD is close to the broken-hearted
>     and saves those who are crushed in spirit.
> (Psalm 34:18)

David knew from personal experience what it was to be broken-hearted and crushed. But he could also testify to the Lord's consolation and comfort even at those times.

So what happens if we don't seem to share that comfort? My problem has been an almost constant sense of God's *absence*. I'd love to sense his closeness. Then, when I think I might be sensing it, I find myself explaining it away by other plausible factors (such as being in a beautiful place, listening to poignant music, enjoying the company of good friends). Of course, I do see all of these as divine gifts – they are all a means of his grace. But I fear I'm missing out, suspecting that these are very different from what others describe and what David sings about. In fact, I even find talk of joy in the Lord quite scary too. That's not because I'm a repressed and cold, stiff-upper-lipped Englishman – those who know me would agree that's not me at all, because my emotions are what we might call 'lively'! It is because I know how fluid and unreliable my emotions are. In fact, that is true of me even before factoring in the black dog's brain blizzards.

So, if I had used my emotional state as a barometer for my spiritual reality, I would have given up years ago. For a start, the very notion of Christian joy would have been exposed as fraudulent – even though I now realize it is not primarily an emotional category at all. I certainly wouldn't be writing this book from the standpoint of Christian faith, let alone Christian ministry. In large part, I can sit here now because of the expectations that were given me at the start, by those who discipled me early on, especially when it comes to what is normal. I'm eternally grateful to them.

Once I learned of Christianity's earliest description, I latched on to it immediately. The first believers are recorded in the book of Acts as having called this new movement 'the Way'. In the original Greek, the word could equally be translated 'path' or 'street' (Acts 9:2; 19:23; 24:24), but it was an ingenious choice. The desire to share what they had discovered in Christ with others was strong from the start. With this word, they could simply invite others to join them on the same road they were walking. That entailed neither superiority nor condescension, but made it clear that just as life is a journey, so too is the experience of trusting Christ. No-one on the Way could claim to have 'made it' or be the finished article. Thus, it had a drawing power best summed up in the adage that defined evangelism as 'simply one beggar showing another beggar where to find bread'.

The significance goes further, though. On this journey, everyone need only go at their own pace. In fact, how can they not? The important thing is always the trajectory that derives from having first encountered God's grace revolution in Christ. The destination of finally being with Christ is what counts, and *not* an individual's speed or efficiency en route. It is a marathon, not a sprint – and the only way to run a marathon (so I am told) is to know your own strength and stamina and set your own pace. Perseverance is the key ingredient. As the writer of Hebrews exhorts, '. . . let us run with perseverance the race marked out for us, fixing our eyes on Jesus, the pioneer and perfecter of faith' (Hebrews 12:1–2).

Unfortunately, listening to some Christians, this marathon metaphor has been dangerously distorted.

At one extreme, the Christian life seems more like a forced march, with everyone regimented in their battalions, constrained by the beat of the drum and the fear of letting down their comrades. This is the mindset that lays down timetables for conversions or victories over sin, one that only gives lip-service to the reality of our weakness or frailty. It is relentlessly activist but exhausting, often driven by leaders with a 'my-way-or-the-highway' approach. It can degenerate into a form of spiritual control, whereby people are kept in check by those who take it upon themselves to humble them (like some fearsome, regimental sergeant major). This is not a pastoral approach that I can find advocated in my Bible, and yet it can be quite prevalent in some churches. Of course, God *does* humble us frequently – but he knows our bigger picture, and his intentions are always good. The same cannot always be said for those who exercise spiritual authority over others. A forced march always leaves weak and broken stragglers behind, casualties of the relentless pace and legalistic activism.

Conversely, the impression can be given that the Christian life is more like a luxury health spa, at which God will provide for all our needs and personal comfort. We need merely to sit back and relax, and let him do the rest. This is the mentality of the old platitudes: 'Let go and let God' or 'Don't wrestle, just nestle!' Of course, if it is a question of encouraging people to trust God to keep his promises, then that is fine, necessary even. But if the suggestion is of life being plain sailing once we meekly 'allow' God to take charge, then we will quickly slip into the fallacy of Job's comforters. All suffering immediately becomes our own fault, in this instance the consequence of lacking sufficient faith.

These are both caricatures, of course. But even hints of these assumptions can be very damaging for those battling mental ill health. In fact, I would go so far as to say that they are damaging for anyone – because they are both constructed on flimsy and false expectations of what God will do for us in this life.

Yet regarding the Christian life as a pilgrimage 'on the Way' liberates us from both conformity (which attempts to create clones or treats everyone as clones) and individualism (which sees spirituality as being like all our other consumer choices, a pick 'n' mix private cocktail of spiritual ideas and fads). We are all individuals, made in God's image but battling with our own different challenges and brokenness; but we are Christ-followers, gathered together on a common pilgrimage, with a common finishing line and 2,000 years of pilgrims' experiences to learn from. We can help each other along the

Way (and indeed, we *need* each other's help) even though each of us is responsible to persevere.

The problem is that there are so many other distortions out there that specifically challenge those pressing on with depression. But since their challenges don't exclusively affect the mentally ill, it is worth outlining them in a little more depth. For, in fact, they help nobody.

## Typical obstacles in the way

### An evangelical prosperity gospel

A disturbing religious phenomenon has swept the world, especially in the Global South. Millions now attend churches in Latin America, Africa and Asia, as well as in the northern hemisphere, which espouse the so-called prosperity gospel. To put it crudely, this promises the riches of heaven to the faithful believer in the here and now, claiming it as the prize for which Christ died. In contexts beset by poverty, corruption and political despair, its appeal is immediate – nothing else seems to alleviate life's drudgery and hopelessness.

Of course, like all heresy, it convinces because it is not entirely false, but masked by apparently biblical foundations. After all, didn't Jesus tell us to pray for 'our daily bread', and that, because our heavenly Father is good, he gives bread (and not stones) when asked? Furthermore, in the old Sinai covenant revealed to Moses, faithfulness to God resulted in blessings in the Promised Land, while inconstancy pro-voked expulsion from the land. This is all explicit in Deuteronomy 28.

It is identical in the new covenant, or so the reasoning goes. Follow Jesus, and he will be lavish in pouring out his riches. Things take an insidious turn when believers are then invited to sow 'seed money' by which they 'invest' for their ultimate blessing. The result is nothing less than a spiritualized pyramid scheme that enriches a handful of pastors and impoverishes the poor still further. What a grotesque distortion of God's kingdom.

The vital missing element is Jesus' call for his followers to take up the cross (Mark 8:34–38). This means a willingness to retrace his footprints to the shame and humiliation of crucifixion as a necessary precursor to the glories of Easter Sunday. He does promise blessing, and indeed the riches of heaven, but these never come at once. We still live in the mess of a broken world; we still battle our sinfulness; we are all flawed, broken and fail. Suffering is a fact of life, side by side with God's consolations and blessings, as Paul knew. But it does not have the final word: 'I consider that our present sufferings are not worth comparing with the glory that will be revealed in us' (Romans 8:18).

This is not to suggest that Paul was in denial about the present, merely that he lived in hope for the promised blessings of life after life:

> We ourselves, who have the firstfruits of the Spirit, groan inwardly as we wait eagerly for our adoption to sonship, the redemption of our bodies. For in this hope we were saved. But hope that is seen is no hope at all. Who hopes for what they already have? But if we hope for what we do not yet have, we wait for it patiently.
> (Romans 8:23–25)

If we follow Christ, we are his disciples and servants and, as such, we cannot expect to fare better than our Teacher and Master.

Yet, despite faithful pastors making its falsehood explicit, so many of us believe deep down that we will somehow cruise through life. Just because we're Christians. Perhaps that is as much a reflection of my privileged background as anything. But I suspect it is more common than that. So many of us have a sneaking presumption that if we have somehow done Jesus a favour by signing up to his team, he therefore owes us a stress-free time. So, if I go to church regularly, if I say my prayers and do good things for other people, then this is all to the good. I'm sure to be fine. I certainly won't get mentally ill. It's all a question of contractual obligations – on both sides.

The problem is that we will be bitterly disappointed soon enough. Our expectations have been distorted into what is effectively a prosperity gospel in all but name. But God doesn't work like that. Instead, he is a God of grace and love, not contracts and just deserts. The whole point of the gospel is that, in Christ, we do *not* get what we deserve. As Matthew Henry, the great seventeenth-century Bible commentator, put it, 'God is a debtor to no man.'[2]

This, of course, means that suffering in this life is a mystery – as we have already seen. It is far more complex a problem than we might like. So being a follower of Christ is no protection from hardship in this life. And in many parts of today's world, it will actually bring hardship. There is, after all, a reason why prosperity gospel teaching has never taken off in the Muslim world.

### The respectability façade

The idea that Christianity was a matter of social conformity and respectability would have made a first-century believer burst out laughing. It's ridiculous! They were despised, jeered at and persecuted. Indeed, for the first three or four centuries of the church's existence at least, that was normality. It persists in many regions to this day.

Yet, in the West, there is still a residue of Christian folk religion whereby it is the done thing to go to church, or rather be seen to go to church. Curiously, it no longer features much in wider UK culture, but *within* church circles, it lingers. There is a strange pressure to put on a good show, a positive face for the outside world to mask any difficulties or anxieties.

It is, therefore, more or less the same kind of middle-class façade that features in many suburban communities. While the lawn and hedgerows out front might be immaculate, it is a different matter entirely behind the front door. There lurk strife and pain. But you would never know it from the topics of conversation. There is no room for frailty. There is certainly no room for error, let alone sin. Not if we want to sustain that all-important good impression. Furthermore, it puts inordinate pressure on ministers and leaders to be something that they are not. It is self-perpetuating, a kind of feedback loop of pretence. Leaders fear opening up about their frailties in case they get crucified by the people who feel let down or even betrayed. This, in turn, affects everyone else. It cuts both ways: a church culture of pretence can be reinforced by how leaders treat those who fail.

Once this syndrome is exposed, it sounds absurd. None of us can possibly maintain it. We are all broken in some way or another. And anyway, it demonstrates a profound misunderstanding of what genuine Christian community should be like. The New Testament is explicit about this: 'Carry each other's burdens, and in this way you will fulfil the law of Christ' (Galatians 6:2); 'Rejoice with those who rejoice; mourn with those who mourn' (Romans 12:15).

How can we bear others' burdens, or weep others' tears, if all pains and troubles are concealed? In a way, any pretence of being 'sorted' deprives the church from being what it was called to be. But, at its worst, an obsession with middle-class respectability is essentially pride that cannot cope with our brokenness. For the depressed person, this is agony. The blizzard might be raging inside, but there is no safety or security outside. The isolating effect of mental illness is thus devastatingly compounded. I begin to believe all the dark and corrosive thoughts that go through the mind. Because everyone around me seems stress-free, then I really must be a freak.

But that's not what church is meant to be like. It is *meant* to be a safe place, where all can find a welcome and a community – regardless of their social awkwardness, psychological hang-ups or identity differences. For the church is our God-given means of persevering together on the Way. Of course, it should never leave us in the same state we were in when we started. But it ought to help us keep the goal in sight, whatever those starting points.

After all, there is not much that is respectable about being a pilgrim. If we are trekking day after day, across different challenging terrains, under fluctuating weather patterns, we will inevitably sweat and weep, and get covered in mud, cuts and bruises. As we walk on, we get tired, we get sick, we get fearful, we get angry, we get sleepy, we get weak. In short, we are stretched to breaking point. And, when we're stretched, the mask inevitably slips. Which is why it's just as well our welcome was not dependent on the appearance of 'sortedness' or respectability. Or at least, it ought not to have been . . .

### Mystery-denying platitudes

One of the most disturbing trends in Western culture recently has been the growth of reductionism.[3] This is the attempt to reduce complexity into soundbites, or just 280 characters, perhaps to make them more memorable, perhaps deliberately to obscure nuance or inconvenient detail. This is not to deny the place for simplicity and clarity. That is an altogether different matter, since these certainly have a legitimate place. After all, it takes deep understanding and mental effort to bring simplicity, and it is any teacher's holy grail.

Speaking simply must not be confused with being simplistic. Yet soundbites claim simplicity while tending towards the simplistic. That is precisely what makes them unhelpful, and is why it is so distressing to find them creeping into everyday church life.

Of course, when people are new to the faith, it is wise to help the first baby steps of faith with aspects that are easier to grasp. Everyone is different, but there is rarely any wisdom in jumping into the theological deep end on day one. I well remember a single-sided help-sheet which gave a few bullet-point answers to the top seven apologetics questions asked by university students. It was an excellent entry point, and genuinely helped to give suggestions for further reflection. I imagine the list would be quite different today, and that I would answer some of the questions slightly differently. Nevertheless, it was useful and greatly used.

However, that sheet could never sustain a lifetime's pilgrimage. It was never designed to. And its entry for the problem of suffering, while helpful, was insultingly brief for someone in the midst of real pain, let alone the cave. Yet if a friend comes along merely parroting the bullet points in the expectation of offering consolation, then it is likely to compound, rather than console, a person's pain.

For example, take the bullet point: 'God uses suffering to discipline and strengthen his children (Romans 5:3–5; Hebrews 12:7–11).' There is profound and necessary truth there. The apostle Paul, for one, taught it, experienced it, testified to its power. Yet it cannot be the whole story, nor does it begin to seek understanding of a person's pain. Which is why it is just as well that there are other bullet points on the sheet – the first of which is crucial: 'We can't know now for sure why God allowed evil into the world.' But that feels like a cop-out unless it is properly worked through.

For example, can God *really* be in control? If he is, then why allow natural disasters? Or individuals to endure mental torment? Or perhaps his power is limited? But if he is sovereign, as is claimed, then it cannot be limited. Which means there is a purpose. But when it causes so much suffering, how can that purpose be good? Or just? Perhaps he isn't either of those things. Or perhaps there isn't, in fact, a purpose – it is just one of those things that happens. In which case, he isn't in control. So round and round it goes. We are left with mystery.

This is why I have been so thankful for C. S. Lewis's brutal candour about his own confusion. It is telling that he most found himself needing to question his deepest convictions only after his beloved wife Joy died of cancer. For in his memoir of bereavement (only published under his own name posthumously), he confesses to his darkest fears about God, terrified he might conclude that he is a 'Cosmic Sadist or Eternal Vivisector':

> Not that I am (I think) in much danger of ceasing to believe in God. The real danger is of coming to believe such dreadful things about Him. The conclusion I dread is not 'So there's no God after all,' but 'So this is what God's really like. Deceive yourself no longer.'[4]

Lewis does not get stuck there, thankfully. He gradually works through grief's pain and confusion – 'No one ever told me that grief felt so like fear',[5] as he famously began – to a renewed, if opaque, confidence in God. Writing the book was, for him, a 'defence against total collapse, a safety-valve, [which] has done some good'.[6]

So, it is clear, one of the twentieth century's greatest Christian minds could not fully resolve all his questions and doubts, even after a hundred or so pages of intense testimony. As he reminisces about one of his last conversations with Joy, when they discussed whether or not she might be able to visit him on *his* deathbed, he stops himself:

> But I mustn't, because I have come to misunderstand a little less completely what a pure intelligence might be, lean over too far. There is also, whatever it means, the resurrection of the body. We cannot understand. The best is perhaps what we understand least.
>
> Didn't people dispute once whether the final vision of God was more an act of intelligence or of love? That is probably another of the nonsense questions.[7]

These are emphatically not the statements of a doubter. They can only be made by someone who believes while profoundly aware of his limits, limits that are most apparent in moments of acute pain. He does not deny the resurrection of the body. He believes that. He just doesn't know what it really means. How can he?

One of the pilgrimage mottos to which I cling most tightly has therefore been Anselm of Canterbury's great adage, 'faith seeking understanding'.[8] In other words, we have some grounds on which to base our trust in God's character and promises, but we don't know everything. We just have enough to go on. And, to be honest, for those in the cave, there are days when even that doesn't *feel* like enough. Isn't this why Paul wrote to the super-spiritual and over-confident Corinthians to put them in their place? 'For now we see only a reflection as in a mirror; then we shall see face to face. Now I know in part; then I shall know fully, even as I am fully known' (1 Corinthians 13:12).

Paul's analogy makes little sense these days, since we expect perfect and clear reflections from our mirrors. However, in the ancient world, they were not made of aluminium-coated glass, but were simply sheets of polished metal, which at best could offer only a blurry and slightly distorted image. So, for example, nobody ever had a reliable sense of their own colouring (which seems hard to imagine in our selfie-obsessed age).

A willingness to persevere along the Way despite life's blurring and incomprehension is a vital ingredient in pilgrim maturity, therefore. We cannot expect to master every theological detail or conundrum in this life. We must be willing to live with the blurs on the metal sheet of our understanding. Not to do so is a fast track to despair. We persevere amidst the mystery (but not the void). So perhaps a great motto prayer for the pilgrim is that of the father of the demon-possessed boy: 'I do believe; help me overcome my unbelief!' (Mark 9:24).

That is, incidentally, why the sight of fellow believers drawing knives over matters of secondary importance, while those of us in the cave are struggling with every fibre of our being to cling to foundational truths, is so dispiriting. There is certainly a place for theological debate, perhaps even heated debate. The New Testament proves that some issues are necessarily divisive. There really *are* genuine gospel issues, which is why I am not advocating a lazy relativism. But when such debate is entertained with a swaggering, self-confident vigour, with the swift vilification and condemnation of opponents, it suggests not only ungodly pride, but also a walk on a very different way. Is this really the talk of someone who accepts that they only 'know in part'? We don't walk in a void – God has revealed himself – but we can't walk on without accepting the inevitability of mystery.

## Stepping gingerly on the Way

Sheffield is a much-loved city in our family, since it is the home of many friends and where both our children were born. During the recent February half-term break, we joined our host for a clamber on the Peak District's crags and rocks a few miles outside the city. The snow cover was thick, as was the swirling, freezing fog. Suddenly, the fact that we had known the paths across Burbage Rocks for twenty years counted for nothing. As we paced along, with dogs clambering in every direction except ours, we unexpectedly reached a cliff edge. We were nowhere near where we thought we were, yet could go no further. So, because it was impossible to figure out what to do in the gloom, we had no alternative but to make our way back to the car.

We might have been pilgrims on the Way for years. We might have taken our understanding to new depths through serious study, even with qualifications and degrees. We might even have been granted responsibilities to care for others, or trusted with significant leadership. But none of it negates the simple fact of being a pilgrim. That means we may well find ourselves stopped in our tracks by something just around the next corner.

In some ways, the whole of life is a string of 'firsts'. First steps; first school; first love; first car accident; first crisis; first child; first public speech; first job; first despair; first public success; first serious illness . . . Each presents a new challenge. The key is to avoid being derailed by applying lessons from past trials or joys to present reality. If the heart of the pilgrim life is to persevere in faith, then we must *decide* to put our trust in him in each new circumstance. But it takes practice. Each will effectively be a 'faith-first' exercise, since we have not had to trust God for this before.

This means that, as we journey on, we have no alternative but to trust him in the face of mental illness. But because each day can feel so different – in fact, brain blizzards can deceive us into thinking each is an unprecedented assault – it means that each also requires a 'faith first'.

## Cheered along the Way: historic predecessors

This is why it is such an encouragement to know we are not the first. Countless others have traced the pilgrim's Way before us.

Throughout the British Isles, many ancient footpaths have been preserved to this day. Often, they were literal pilgrim routes to sites such as Canterbury Cathedral in Kent, or to Lindisfarne in Northumberland along St Cuthbert's Way (which starts in Selkirk in Scotland). I have never followed an entire route, but have occasionally walked along small sections – my favourite probably being the North Downs Way (from Winchester to Canterbury), a part of which is actually known as The Pilgrims' Way. It is deeply moving to plant one's feet on matted or muddied tracks in the full knowledge that countless thousands have been doing precisely that for *hundreds* of years. In all weathers. In all circumstances. On paths that have not changed.

This is one reason why the Bible constantly reminds us of our spiritual predecessors. The writer to the Hebrews famously does this in his faith heroes' portrait gallery (in chapter 11). But his main purpose in describing the gallery can be overlooked. Notice how he continues:

Therefore, since we are surrounded by such a great cloud of witnesses, let us throw off everything that hinders and the sin that so easily entangles. And let us run with perseverance the race marked out for us, fixing our eyes on Jesus, the pioneer and perfecter of faith. For the joy that was set before him he endured the cross, scorning its shame, and sat down at the right hand of the throne of God. Consider him who endured such opposition from sinners, so that you will not grow weary and lose heart.

(Hebrews 12:1–3)

The Christian pilgrimage – or to pick up Hebrews' analogy here, the marathon – is not without its banks of supporters cheering their people on from the stands. This audience is unusual, though, because every single one of them has finished the race – they know exactly what it takes. For, if you scan through the gallery, it's clear that they have persevered through unimaginable things: crime, war, torture, oppression, exile and persecution. As he says, 'the world was not worthy of them' (Hebrews 11:38). But they're now cheering us on with gusto. Their memories only make them shout their encouragements all the louder!

What is true of saints of old is also true of saints we have known. I can recall several believers, including my grandparents, who have now been 'promoted to glory', to use that quaint but rather marvellous Salvation Army phrase. Their faith has inspired me to persevere. Even more affecting is to imagine them having just found their seats in the stands, and adding their voices to the resounding cheers of that throng of heavenly spectators. Sometimes it is worth stopping to consider each one, specifically recalling what it was about them that was so helpful or encouraging – and then simply giving thanks to God for the privilege of knowing them.

But there is one who eclipses them all, the one who pioneered it all – Jesus himself. He called us to follow him in the first place, to take up our own cross as he did (Mark 8:34–38). That is why it is such comfort to read that not only is he the pioneer of our faith, but the perfecter as well. He enables it to happen. So we fix our eyes on him.

Yet a problem remains. What actually does that mean in practice? How do we focus on one who cannot be seen?

## Led along the Way: taking it on trust

Some years ago, I was speaking at a December conference in Skopje, Macedonia. On the day of my scheduled departure, the entire city was swathed in impenetrable fog, a pea-souper of the kind that London used to know in the 1950s. I'd never experienced anything quite like it – a combination of freezing temperatures, a microclimate created by encircling mountains, and the noxious fumes of vehicle pollution. It was a lethal cocktail. My primary problem, however, was the total closure of the airport until it lifted. I was grounded for three extra days. All was not lost – thankfully, the airline put me up in a hotel, while I got to enjoy the gift of unexpectedly free days with dear friends. But it was frustrating, nonetheless.

I had always assumed that modern aircraft were equipped with sensitive guidance systems specifically designed for this kind of scenario. But when the visibility gets this bad, even the best technology is insufficiently reliable. It's all a matter of whom or what you trust in the end. Of course, most of us are inclined to trust our own perceptions and perspectives by default. That is the reason why we so often find ourselves at dead ends or in confusion – as we did on our Peak District walk. We need a more reliable guide.

The question is – who can we trust to guide us in this world? It's a terrifying question for someone with mental illness. Because we know our perceptions have been warped and distorted. Where do we turn when we're blind and deaf?

Because most of us are not sight impaired, the incongruity does not register, but so much of our language of comprehension is made up of sight metaphors. For example, when the penny drops, we say, 'Oh yes, I see what you mean.' Or, if we express an opinion, we might say, 'Well, as I see things . . .' To see means to understand. And worse, for many, if something can't be seen, it can't be true. That has been a serious problem for Christian apologetics in recent decades – because, of course, Christian discipleship is founded on invisible realities.

For understandable reasons, the Corinthian Christians wanted visible evidence for their beliefs. Who doesn't? They wanted something impressive to show for their trust in Christ, no doubt to reassure themselves and to convince sceptical friends. But Paul is adamant. 'We live by faith, not by sight,' he says (2 Corinthians 5:7). We have no alternative. In other words, we must take the route of the Way on trust. Even when it looks wrong. Or, perhaps, especially when it looks wrong.

But what does that mean?

We must start by assessing the wisdom of trusting Christ's perspective. Is he reliable? Faith is no medical condition that one either has or doesn't have; nor is it a question of launching out into the void in complete ignorance. The future is unknown, for sure, but as one of the twentieth century's great heroes of the faith, Corrie ten Boom, discovered, we should never weary of 'trusting an unknown future to a known God'. She suffered terribly in a Nazi concentration camp for her family's courageous protection of Dutch Jews – and yet still testified to the truth of that statement.

Living by faith not sight depends on an internal dialogue, a case review if you like, in which we have to remind ourselves why this might be the sensible path. In the midst of mystery or confusion (especially when it comes to mental illness), it always comes back to the character of God as revealed in Christ. For he did say to Thomas, 'If you really know me, you will know my Father as well' (John 14:7).

- Has God revealed himself sufficiently trustworthy to enable perseverance in the fog? Does he have a track record of reliability?

That entails several other sub-questions:

- What happened when I, or others, trusted God's way?
- Were there times when God's way was not as it seemed?
- How do we manage at those times?

This explains why my most thumbed chapters of the Bible during cave times (after the Psalms) are in the four Gospels. For there I am reminded afresh what Jesus was actually like. In particular, I see how he treated those who struggled or were marginalized, those whom the world casts out or fails to comprehend. He is gentle, tender and wise. This is not to say he is permissive or morally lax – his is the way of transformative grace, as he beautifully demonstrates with the so-called woman caught in adultery (John 8:1–11). Furthermore, he gives short shrift to those who hypocritically project themselves as having everything sorted with God. But, all the time, he has a magnetism that is especially attractive for those battling with mental health.

More important than any of that, however, is his resolution to walk the way of the cross. For example, as early as Luke

9:51, he 'resolutely set out for Jerusalem', in full recognition of what would occur there. Nothing would deter him. But every step along the Way was hard. We can only guess at the psychological and spiritual cost of that journey, although the closest glimpse we have comes in Gethsemane only hours before his execution. There he is gripped by such stress and fear that his brow drips with sweat, and capillaries burst. But still he can say, 'Not my will, but yours' (Luke 22:39–44). This is the way of faith – trusting in God's good purposes in the darkest of nights, when emotions are wrought and perspectives completely distorted. This is living by faith, not by sensory perception.

Imagine being a visitor to Jerusalem that fateful Passover week. You hear about the public executions that are to take place that Friday, beyond the city boundaries, and it just so happens that these crucifixions are held on the route you need to go home. The charges are placed above each criminal. The middle one is laughable – 'the king of the Jews'? It's a sick joke. Fantasist claimants to the crown end up on crosses, not thrones. God's will? It can't be.

And yet . . .

In God's kingdom, appearances are invariably deceptive. What we perceive with our senses is not a reliable guide to what God is doing. As Paul implied to the Corinthians, appearance and reality do not necessarily conform.

> We preach Christ crucified: a stumbling-block to Jews and foolishness to Gentiles, but to those whom God has called, both Jews and Greeks, Christ the power of God and the wisdom of God. For the foolishness of God is wiser than human wisdom, and the weakness of God is stronger than human strength.
>
> (1 Corinthians 1:23–25)

He is being provocative in suggesting that God might be considered foolish or weak – that seems utterly incongruous. But Paul's point is that God is only foolish or weak when judged by human criteria. On those terms, the cross will never make sense. It is only through the lens of trust in God's interpretation (revealed here through Paul) that we see beyond the perceptible. We see that the Way of Good Friday does ultimately lead to the victory and glory of Easter Sunday. The problem is that the doldrums of Easter Saturday cannot be bypassed.

Of course, we live this side of Easter – we know (on trust) that Christ has risen and is alive. So our circumstances are not identical. But I do sometimes wonder if the spiritual pain of mental illness is akin to the bewilderment of that middle Saturday. The disciples had Christ's words about his resurrection (for example, Mark 8:31; 9:31; 10:33–34) – but having witnessed his execution, these seemed hollow. All was bleak and hopeless. No wonder those two on the Emmaus road were leaving town, because they 'had hoped that he was the one who was going to redeem Israel' (Luke 24:21). That was *in spite of* the women's report of an empty tomb (Luke 24:22–24)! It took an extraordinary encounter with the risen Jesus to stop them in their tracks and send them hurtling back to Jerusalem.

There have been many days when I have prayed for such an encounter with Christ. Or, at least, to have greater consolations of his grace in depression's fog. But, for reasons only he can know, it has not happened like that. I have had to cling to the track record, to the knowledge that he is a reliable friend on the Way. He has been there ahead of me. He expects of his followers nothing less than what he has done himself, like all the best leaders. And what he did achieve, he did for us all. I take that on trust – I live by faith, not sight.

But when engulfed by the swirling billows of freezing fog, that is the only thing we can do.

Jesus is therefore not only one in whom we begin walking along the Way, nor is he simply the goal of the Way. He also accompanies us along the way. Perhaps that explains why one of my favourite verses from any hymn is the final verse of John E. Bode's 'O Jesus, I Have Promised' (written in 1868):

O let me see thy footmarks,
and in them plant mine own;
My hope to follow duly
is in thy strength alone.
O guide me, call me, draw me,
uphold me to the end;
and then in heaven receive me,
my Saviour and my Friend.

## 8. THE FELLOW-TRAVELLERS

An obvious question flowing out of the previous chapter might be: 'Why is there still a problem, then? After all, if your experience reflects normal Christian living, and you accept that, why not just persevere and be done with it? Why make such a fuss of all this black dog stuff?'

Well, it would be fine if human beings were as logical and programmable as machinery. But we're not. Thankfully. Life and society would be numbingly dull if we were. As many have noted, when human beings freeze water, we make ice cubes; when God freezes water, he makes snowflakes. Each one is unique, the potential for variations infinite. If Christian maturity is a matter of growing in Christlikeness, with the unique combination of personality, temperament and circumstances that each of us experiences, then each of us has our own unique path to walk. However – and this is crucial – having unique burdens and joys is never the grounds for going it alone. Which is a relief. I can't do this alone. And nobody said that I needed to.

On my better days, I can somehow 'talk down' the blizzard. I've never stood at the helm of an English Channel ferry during a gale and told it to shut up, as Jesus did on Lake Galilee. I have a pretty good idea of how ineffective that would be and how stupid I would look. But I can calm my internal storms with a voice. That is nothing short of miraculous! Perhaps, to be more accurate, I don't always find that the storm completely evaporates (although it can do). I work my mind through to a point of living with the inner turmoil and then, somehow, sitting light to it. It is usually a question of reviewing (again . . . and again . . . and again . . .) my knowledge of reality as opposed to my perceptions of it. In short, I must preach to myself.

I just wish the better days were more frequent. It does seem to be a cyclical thing, and I can go through periods of greater stability, and then suddenly (without warning or even obvious catalysts) plunge into instability. It defies logic – it can occur even in places where I 'should' be better off. Places with happy memories, family (or friend) gatherings, even times of success or fulfilment are no bar to recurrences. Perhaps this is the one area where the use of 'depression' language is appropriate, because a weather system depression can sometimes appear as suddenly as it dissipates.

I have always loved a sketch by British comedy duo Mel Smith and Griff Rhys Jones. I haven't been able to find it online, but if I remember correctly, Griff is taking a driving test, while Mel is in the passenger seat, tapping his clipboard with a biro. They come to a T-junction where Griff stops the car, and then he looks left and right, left and right to check the coast is clear. The terrain is flat and he can see for miles in every direction. There isn't a vehicle in sight. Mel says, 'In your own time . . .' But still the nervous driver peers from side to side. Then, without warning, a Ford Transit van plummets out of the sky and squashes the car flat. A tumble into the blizzard can feel as unexpected and absurd as that.

So on those worse days . . . ? I lack the energy to preach to, let alone hear, myself. It's not laziness. It's exhaustion from fighting the blizzard. For mental illness doesn't simply make living the Christian life difficult; it makes living difficult.

### Reality touchstones

Occasionally, my children get so engrossed in a book or series that they want us to join in the fun. Suzanne Collins' Hunger Games trilogy was a case in point. We were all gripped, and enjoyed the books much more than the films (although these could have been much worse)! The trilogy's themes were thought-provoking and insightful about contemporary culture in ways that I really did not expect from so-called 'young adult' fiction. One aspect, however, really struck me as holding huge pastoral significance.

In the final book, *Mockingjay*, Peeta Mellark is reunited with his oldest ally, Katniss. Without spoiling the plot unduly, Peeta has suffered intolerably at the hands of the Capitol's torturers. They have crippled his perceptions irreversibly with mind-altering poisons, jettisoning him into relentless disorientation. This causes him to treat those who love him most with hostility and aggression. It is heartbreaking, since, before this point, he was the books' kindest and most sympathetic character. Now he must navigate this new normal.

Naturally, his closest friends are hurt and wary because they can't fully understand what has happened to him. But, thankfully, Katniss and Peeta find a way to cope. It requires extravagant patience on her part, immense trust on his. But after everything they have endured – and we are to believe they are still only teenagers! – it is clear that survival can only come from mutual dependence. Peeta must allow himself to lean on Katniss's more reliable perceptions of reality. He happens on a deceptively simple question:

> 'You're still trying to protect me. Real or not real?' he whispers.
>   'Real,' I answer. It seems to require more explanation.
> 'Because that's what you and I do. Protect each other.' After
> a minute or so, he drifts off to sleep.[1]

The Capitol's poisons seem not a million miles from mental illness. It follows, therefore, that one of the most precious gifts to someone with depression, or any mental affliction for that matter, is to be a reality touchstone, as Katniss was to Peeta. Real, or not real? It's the most important question. I weep for those who lack any such touchstone. For theirs truly is a living hell.

The Christian pilgrimage was always meant to be walked with others, because every single one of us (however mentally resilient) has bad days. The writer to the Hebrews, unsurprisingly, had words for 'go-it-alone' believers:

> Let us consider how we may spur one another on towards love
> and good deeds, not giving up meeting together, as some are
> in the habit of doing, but encouraging one another – and all
> the more as you see the Day approaching.
> (Hebrews 10:24–25)

If that is the case, how much more vital is it for walkers on the Way who struggle to distinguish between the 'real or not real'?

## Encounters within the cave

Mental illness is such an isolating phenomenon. That is why the analogy of the dark, dank cave works so well for me. It is impossible to explain the workings (or rather lack of them) of an individual mind to another person. But we can resonate with the words of others who appear to experience something similar. In fact, there is nothing quite like the moment of finding that the cave you are in is not as uninhabited as you first thought. Others may not live in exactly the same chamber, but they are nearby, sometimes uncannily so. It's like being in a foreign country and suddenly meeting someone from home.

In the summer before university, my oldest mate Ollie and I went Interrailling. Using a single month-long ticket, it's possible to travel on any train in Europe, and so is a wonderfully cheap way to see new places. Because of our mild obsession with the classical world, we decided to focus the entire trip on Italy. Long before smartphones and Google, we formed plans on the hoof, making impulse decisions according to the most intriguing destinations on station departure boards. This did lead to one or two more chaotic moments, however. One evening, we found ourselves hope-lessly lost on the backstreets of Milan, without a clue where we were going to stay that night. We had only the most basic tourist map of the city, but we were emphatically not in a touristy area. Then the weirdest thing happened. We turned the corner from one unexceptional street to another just as it was getting dark, only to bump into someone from my year at school. We hadn't known each other well, but we did at least know each other's names. Most importantly, he could tell us where to find a nearby hostel, as well as the city centre. It was extraordinary. What he was doing in that part of Milan I have no idea, because we really were far from the beaten track. But that chance encounter liberated us from a miserable night!

Meeting other cave-dwellers can be like that – especially if they've been there longer than we have. They know where to find food and shelter. This is the joy of shared experience, and leads to the deepest friendship and bonds already considered. This is why I love Ruby Wax's description of others in the cave as 'my people'. I know exactly what she means.

So time with others in the cave is invaluable and precious. It can hold us back from the precipice. It reminds us that we are not as alone as we feared, and that our experiences are more normal than we believed. It so often takes another cave-dweller to play Katniss, to show me where I've got the 'real' horribly confused with the 'not real'. I appreciate my fellow cave-dwellers so, so much.

There can, however, be limits. For the risk of dragging one another down is a genuine one. It is not inevitable, of course, especially if our own depression follows a cyclical pattern and we are in a less vulnerable moment. But we need care and wisdom, and I would certainly not advocate the formation of a commune of cave-dwellers (not one without good pastoral leadership, that is). This is because we can identify with each others' pains *too* much. Our shared experiences create a natural empathy, which makes it hard not to be affected by another's state of mind. It is almost contagious! I find that I am most prone to being negatively affected when I'm on a downward slide, or already close to the bottom. Another's experience serves only to accelerate the decline or deepen the pit. If one's mental state is adversely affected by circumstances or current affairs (as mine is), then this can be an acute problem. So, paradoxically, it may be the case that fellow cave-dwellers are not the best people to help, if they are as disoriented about reality as we are.

So there is a tightrope to walk here. It is as much about knowing ourselves and our own limits as anything. I could not do without my fellow cave-dwellers, but it is vital to identify where one's emotional boundaries lie. There are times when it would not be helpful to pick up the phone or reply to that email. There will be other opportunities to do that. I need to remember that I am not indispensable, and that self-care may include temporary withdrawal.

This is, in part, why we need those outside the cave as well. Especially when they have the Katniss gift. The challenge is not only finding them, but also trusting them . . .

## Wary of others outside the cave

How is it possible to counteract the cave's muffling effect? Those closest to us long to find ways to help and connect, because they love us and are witnessing what is so evidently painful.

It must start with grasping why the cave is so isolating, since only then will it be possible to begin to counteract its effects.

### In the cave because of the stigma

Those in the cave feel isolated, because there is stigma related to mental illness, perhaps especially (though not exclusively) for men. I am more fortunate than many in that I have not felt this acutely. I have never been asked to resign from a job, or to keep a low profile, or to refrain from mentioning it. But this says as much about the generation I was born into as it does of the people I have had the privilege of working with.

It would have been a different matter if I had been born thirty years earlier, say, or if I lived within different cultural contexts. I have heard horror stories of how some are treated. One African brother was informed by his board chairman that the reason why he was struggling was because he was lazy. It was his laziness that had caused his burn-out, apparently. Go figure.

So, in another context, I could easily have been accused of lacking stickability or backbone or 'moral fibre' (whatever that is). I might have been passed over for jobs as an unreliable sort, or had responsibilities unilaterally removed. I might have been deemed unfit for Christian ministry because of it.

The essence of the problem is that there is nothing *to see*. A broken leg in plaster is obvious. It might elicit some good-humoured jokes, requests to sign the cast and, hopefully, sympathy (especially if people notice a struggle to perform mundane tasks like climbing a staircase). At the very least, most people will make allowances for a physical ailment.

But mental health? It's doubtful. Imagine the responses when someone is asked to do something and they reply, 'I'm really sorry but I'm really battling with anxiety about doing that.' It sounds like a pathetic excuse, a weakness or cop-out, or, to take that excruciating epithet so frequently bandied about at my boarding school, 'rather wet'. But what if it genuinely does lead to some of those physical repercussions discussed in chapter 2? They might not be visible as such, but they are real enough. What if a routine ministry task suddenly has that effect, especially if it has never caused any difficulties previously? After all, it is many people's nightmare scenario: speaking and acting in public, under the relentless, and occasionally hypercritical, gaze of those who have seen many do it competently before.

Ministry is a tough call for anyone. In its contemporary forms, however, it makes unique demands on leaders, many of which never even occur to those they serve. After comparing notes with friends and colleagues, there is clearly a potentially lethal cocktail of stressors:

- Pastoral roles are often best suited to those who are more extroverted, and yet the individuals drawn to those roles are usually more introverted.
- The nature of pastoral ministry is that it is isolating (for example, because of the need for confidentiality, facts of geography, or the requirement to take tough leadership decisions), and yet it invariably involves very complex and emotionally draining issues. The problem is compounded by how rarely pastors make use of external pastoral supervision.
- Churches habitually expect ministers to display an omni-competence: to be powerful public speakers, sensitive pastoral counsellors, effective budget managers, ebullient social organizers, the life and soul of the party.

So what happens if a minister suddenly feels 'not up to it' this time? Must the pain simply be ignored, like a marathon runner experiencing the twenty-mile 'wall'? Is it a matter of setting faces like flint and ploughing on? What happens if this weakness is shared? Is that disqualifying?

So some, perhaps many, will keep quiet rather than risk the humiliation and scorn, even to their own detriment. C. S. Lewis recognized that all too well:

> Mental pain is less dramatic than physical pain, but it is more common and also more hard to bear. The frequent attempt to conceal mental pain increases the burden: it is easier to say 'My tooth is aching' than to say 'My heart is broken.'[2]

The net effect is, therefore, to isolate the isolated sufferer still further, in a way that somehow cements up any cave openings that might have existed. The cave has now become a cell.

### In the cave because it's so foreign

It is unlikely, although not impossible, that our family, closest friends and colleagues will respond with that kind of hardship. My experience is that we feel separated from those closest to us because there seems so little to connect our pain with their understanding. We grope for the words, we want the sympathy and, more importantly, the empathy, and so we blurt things out. But it doesn't do justice to it, nor does it seem to help to build a bridge.

Our friends get frustrated and hurt by our introversion and selfishness (which, let's face it, can be a fair charge). They are inevitably juggling other demands and pains of their own. If we are prickly, then it is natural that they read this as grounds for withdrawal. They tried to help, but to no avail.

So we are left alone. In one sense, that is less painful than the incomprehension or lack of empathy. But it is not ideal – especially when we lose a sense of the 'real'. The cave then becomes one's totality. Connections beyond it don't seem possible.

### In the cave because of 'dementors'

When J. K. Rowling created the Harry Potter universe, she naturally drew on her own experiences to flesh it out. This is true even for such alarming creatures as 'dementors'. These are soulless beings that stand at around 3 metres, constantly breathing in a human being's positive emotions and memories of others, such that their victims relive only the worst. Intriguingly, Rowling has said that they 'grow like fungi in dark, moist places, creating a dense, chilly fog', which makes it sound remarkably as though their natural habitat is a cave! This serves to make them effective guards at Azkaban prison.[3]

It is no surprise to learn, therefore, that Rowling's inspiration for the dementors was her own period of clinical depression. They are a brilliant personification of its effects.

The tragedy, just occasionally, is that others can have a dementor-like effect on us. I would never stoop to the suggestion of anyone being soulless. I also fully appreciate that each of us bears our own deep scars. The oft-repeated adage puts it well: be kind, for everyone you meet is fighting a battle you know nothing about. On reflection, it is probably not repeated enough.

Nevertheless, a handful of individuals in the past twenty-five years have had this effect on me. I emerge from each encounter depleted and despairing. Their interactions reinforce the news-ticker negativity that perpetually scrolls through my head. I believe that stuff more when I'm with them. My instinct is to flee and hide, to curl into foetal protection.

These individuals were exceptions. Nobody else has had quite that effect on me. But occasionally, moments and conversations, even with friends, have. The net result is obvious. The cave then becomes one's refuge.

## Coaxing out of the cave

It may be that you are reading this as one who loves a cave-dweller deeply. I thank God for you. Seriously. More than anything in the world, loved ones are the key to survival. But perhaps you feel at sea. Nothing you say or do seems to help. You feel as if you only aggravate or irritate, or even drive those suffering deeper underground. Nevertheless, it is vital, as friends, to persevere.

The book of Proverbs offers a rich mine for considering friendship. Because its writers had no illusions about life's messiness, it is especially helpful here. They have much to say about choosing friends and, by inference, about being friends. What is clear, however, is the importance of sticking at it. That is the hallmark of true friendship, par excellence. Friends are not diverted from their commitments by anything:

> A friend loves at all times,
>     and a brother is born for a time of adversity.
> (Proverbs 17:17)

The writers knew how revealing times of hardship can be for our relationships. They were unequivocal about fair-weather friends:

> Wealth attracts many friends,
>     but even the closest friend of the poor person
>         deserts them . . .
> Many curry favour with a ruler,
>     and everyone is the friend of one who gives gifts.
> (Proverbs 19:4, 6)

They had clearly seen what goes wrong when people choose their friendship circles unwisely:

> One who has unreliable friends soon comes to ruin,
>     but there is a friend who sticks closer than a brother.
> (Proverbs 18:24)

There is no finer ambition than to be a friend with this kind of fraternal stickability. The problem, though, is that we might want to 'love at all times', but we just don't know how.

I wish I could give more concrete suggestions, but can only speak of what have been my own longings or lifesavers.

It comes down to just three words: presence, persistence, reassurance.

### *Presence*

This is where Job's friends got it right initially. They simply met with this overwhelmed, broken soul in companionable silence, on the very ash-heap where he sat scraping the dirt out of his aching sores. It was a pitiful scene. They wept with him and sat with him *for a whole week* (Job 2:8, 11–13). In contrast to so many, they moved *towards* another's pain instead of recoiling from it. That takes guts by itself. It is a remarkable act, for which Eliphaz, Bildad and Zophar deserve great credit, at least. It would have been emotionally exhausting and costly. What's more, they resisted the urge to speak.

Silence is scarce in today's world, but it is so precious. Its absence is one possible reason why it feels so threatening. Wherever we go, it seems that we must be accompanied by music, advertising, tannoy announcements, general chatter and hubbub. We can't even escape being serenaded in public toilets. This makes it even harder for modern people to resist plugging every conversation gap with something else. It takes practice to hold back.

My problem is that I am all too aware of another's awkwardness with silence. I can pick up on any anxieties about saying the wrong thing or feeling helpless. That can then be counterproductive, ironically making matters harder. So, even though being a good friend is not exactly a matter of skills to study, it is possible to invest in learning how this can be done better. We can do a lot worse than developing an ease and a contentedness with silence. Practise using the time to reflect on life, to pray and praise, to read, and ultimately just to 'be'. That must be a beneficial exercise in our 24/7 culture anyway. I, for one, enjoy the companionship of being in a room with others while we all just read our books!

For I have found that I most want others 'to be' for me, rather than 'to do' for me. I long for them to have the confidence to know that their friendship *in and of itself* brings healing, that I don't need their answers or action plans. If I did, I would ask for them – and sometimes I do. I wish they knew that feeling helpless is actually OK – at least it demonstrates an awareness of the affliction's nature! And it is fair to say that sharing silence with a friend will *never* by itself do harm, and may well do great good. That seems counter-intuitive because of its apparent passivity. But I do believe that it is a profound act of love, simply because someone else's time is such a precious gift. Especially these days. American novelist Margaret Runbeck captured the paradox well: 'Silences make the real conversations between friends. Not the saying but the never needing to say is what counts.'

However, it is also true that physical presence may not literally be what is needed (which will come as a relief to those who have little time to spare). For someone in the cave, it is as good to know that a friend is constantly there. Solitude (which should not be confused with loneliness) can be helpful at times, especially for those who are more introverted. But, at those points, it is vital to be reminded that, even when I am out of sight, I am not out of mind. So a friend's presence might simply amount to a regular text message to 'check in', to ask how the day is, for example. That's not so difficult, surely. Some might worry that's just a token gesture. But I would *far* rather have gestures than absence. Without gestures, my mind spins ever darker explanations from my own failures.

At its heart, this is a question of relationship quality and trust. This is why the next aspect is crucial. It is also the toughest.

### Persistence

I am horribly ashamed to admit how abominably I have treated my friends at times. In thankfully rare moments of desperation, I have lashed out in fury, ranting in expletive-filled streams of consciousness. I suppose that might be preferable to the passive stupor associated with depression, because it attests to flickers of life. But it is scant consolation to those on the receiving end. Thankfully, as I've said, this has not happened too often – it is more likely that they have experienced my hedgehog impressions, curling up until only the prickles are visible.

I understand fully those who find it hard to deal with this behaviour – not least because they are fighting invisible battles that only get exacerbated by such rebuffs. I genuinely do not regard this as a failing of friendship, even if I occasionally feel like it is. But in this situation, it is surely the duty of friendship to ensure that some *are* persevering with the afflicted. It is vital to have at least a few who can see past the brush-offs.

Patience and grace are the name of the game here – especially if we're at the thirty-seventh hearing of the pain. There is no need to put on the extra sympathetic face and deeper, burdened tone.

Asking questions, perhaps surprisingly, is also crucial. But do so carefully. It is vital to avoid the Job's comforter syndrome, whereby one probes to get at the roots of the suffering so as to satisfy one's own theological framework. Furthermore, asking questions is not an opportunity to road-test any psychotherapeutic ambitions or have a stab at amateur diagnosis on the back of a couple of interesting blogposts. It may be that the best help a friend can offer is to point the way to a professional therapist, if this is needed – and in my experience, it usually is. But a friend's most important asset is the most obvious: simple, accepting friendship. Come what may.

The purpose of gentle enquiry is simple – to show interest in the cave-dweller, to seek understanding, to help him or her to feel heard. In fact, others' attempted understanding (however imperfect) is what I have craved more than anything. Especially when I didn't really understand what was happening myself. Throughout the cave experience, others' attempts to understand has been the surest way of feeling valued.

So ask open-ended questions. Gently probe the person's experience to find anything that connects. Even if you can't find them, offer analogies as they occur to you, but move on quickly if they don't resonate. Here are a few simple suggestions to give the general gist:

- What makes it so hard right now?
- What more would you like to add to what you said the other day?
- What do you wish others understood?
- Is it like trying to hear yourself think next to a traffic junction, or something else?
- Are there times of day that are worse than others or is it more general than that?
- How has meeting others with similar pain helped you?
- How might trying to write your experiences down help?

Notice the focus here: it's far more a matter of description than diagnosis. Attempting this surely lifts much of the pressure, because most of us don't have anything like the skills or training to do more than that. It means anyone can be a good friend. If willing. I cannot tell you how wonderful it is to encounter this. Writer and actor Stephen Fry was absolutely right:

> If you know someone who's depressed, please resolve never to ask them why. Depression isn't a straightforward response to a bad situation; depression just is, like the weather.
>
> Try to understand the blackness, lethargy, hopelessness, and loneliness they're going through. Be there for them when they come through the other side. It's hard to be a friend to someone who's depressed, but it is one of the kindest, noblest, and best things you will ever do.[4]

It is worth saying that good friends need to decide *in advance* never to be shocked or thrown. This is not to suggest appearing unaffected or unmoved, nor to deny the possibility of shocking and difficult things being said. Indeed, these may well require some sort of action to be taken. But it is vital not to panic or show alarm during the conversation. For the only way to coax someone out of the cave is to offer space that is safe and secure.

Finally, despite everything so far, it may well be that there are actually things to *do*. Everyone is different, and nothing should be imposed, only offered. Talk about it!

This is a far from exhaustive list:

- **Pray!** And perhaps send a text to say what you particularly prayed for. The cave's deepest recesses somehow make prayer impossible. That's one of its cruellest hallmarks. Sometimes it was even unbearable to hear someone praying for me – perverse and absurd though that sounds. Please don't condemn that – but pray on regardless. Perhaps use the psalmist's prayers for himself as a steer.

- **Share**: it's not everyone's cup of tea, so it is always a matter of knowing friends well. But sharing a song, a poem, a line, a verse – anything really – that you find helpful yourself can be wonderful. Don't be didactic, though. Avoid things that 'they jolly well ought to have realized by now'. And don't be offended if what you share doesn't connect.

- **Accompany**: even though I have found therapy to be lifesaving at times, I still find myself descending as an appointment draws near. I have rarely needed someone to help me do this, but I know it can be so helpful. So offer to go along to an appointment, saying you're happy just to sit in the waiting room. That speaks volumes. Or perhaps it is simply a matter of keeping an eye out in a crowd in case some protection is helpful, such as at coffee time after church or in the canteen at work.

- **Hospitality**: to have friends share their home, while making clear it comes without expectations of being sparkling company, can be liberating. Just offering a 'normal' environment, while family chaos continues all around, is such a gift. Please don't invite others along without agreeing on it, though, even with the best of motives.

Above all, whatever you do offer, don't give up on doing it.

### Reassurance

One hallmark of friendship highlighted by the book of Proverbs is time spent in conversation. It *may* be a matter of sharing advice and experience:

Perfume and incense bring joy to the heart,
    and the pleasantness of a friend
    springs from their heartfelt advice.
(Proverbs 27:9)

Yet even more significant perhaps is the willingness to say difficult or unpalatable things. In fact, such willingness should be regarded as definitive:

Wounds from a friend can be trusted,
    but an enemy multiplies kisses.
(Proverbs 27:6)

It is precisely because friends are motivated by love that they should be trusted. A bogus sycophant is as worthless as a fair-weather friend.

But when it comes to supporting cave-dwellers, caution is crucial. A wounding, accusatory or challenging word, however well-intentioned or apparently necessary, merely twists the knife still further. It is not even a question of thinking twice before saying such things – I would strongly urge avoiding doing so altogether, unless circumstances really make it necessary. Otherwise, you will only compound the guilt and shame explored in earlier chapters. I have been on the receiving end of such words, and they have probably driven me closer to the edge than anything else.

Then, there are some lines that should be removed from your pastoral phrase book at all costs:

- Why can't you just snap out of it?
- Just think positive – none of this negativity helps anyone.

- Confess your sins, and this will all go away.
- Take your pills, and it'll be fine / you must stop your pills because they're dragging you down.
- He / she / I has / have been through far worse – what are you complaining about?
- God won't give you more than you can handle.
- It's sinful to be joyless / anxious / frightened / lose perspective.

Instead, a good friend takes note of the emotional temperature. I have always loved this proverb because it perfectly captures those who fail to do this (and it is surely worth bearing in mind if you plan church worship services):

> Like one who takes away a garment on a cold day,
>> or like vinegar poured on a wound,
>> is one who sings songs to a heavy heart.
> (Proverbs 25:20)

Think. Listen. Pray. Ask yourself, 'What does *this* heavy heart most need from me right *now*?'

This is where words of reassurance come in. If the fog has descended, and reality has been distorted or entirely obscured, then a friend's greatest gift is to be a counterbalance. To be a Katniss to a Peeta. To offer perspective where it is evaporating, to offer alternative interpretations where only the darkest appear to make sense.

Therapists helpfully refer to the problem of catastrophizing. This is a tendency to accept only the worst explanations for something, or to believe that the most terrible outcomes are possible, and even inevitable. It is especially common in those who have experienced trauma or tragedy. It makes sense because they have known catastrophe, and so, not unreasonably, fear its repetition. But it makes everything get out of proportion.

So one way to reassure is to open up the possibility of other interpretations, to talk us down from believing the worst. To be the person who can say 'real' or 'not real'. It might be a matter of gently offering alternative explanations for not hearing from someone in a while, or simple reminders of the wonders of unshakeable gospel grace, or just a silent arm around the shoulder. Anything really.

## Escape from Doubting Castle

We have already encountered John Bunyan's pilgrims, Christian and Hopeful, languishing in Giant Despair's dungeon without hope of release (back in chapter 3). But the story does not end there. The manner of their escape from their dementor's clutches is startling but instructive:

> Well, on Saturday, about midnight, they began to pray, and continued in prayer till almost break of day.
>
> Now a little before it was day, good Christian, as one half-amazed, did break out into this passionate speech:
>
> CHRISTIAN: What a fool am I, to lie in a stinking dungeon, when I may as well walk at liberty! I have a key in my bosom called Promise, that will, I am persuaded, open any lock in Doubting Castle.
>
> HOPEFUL: That's good news; good brother, pluck it out of thy bosom, and try.
>
> Then Christian pulled it out of his bosom and began to try at the dungeon door, whose bolt, as he turned the key, gave back, and the door flew open with ease, and Christian and Hopeful both came out. Then he went to the outward door that leads into the castle yard and with his key opened that

door also. After that he went to the iron gate, for that must be opened too; but that lock went desperately hard, yet the key did open it.

Now when they were gone over the stile, they began to contrive with themselves what they should do at that stile, to prevent those that shall come after from falling into the hands of Giant Despair. So they consented to erect there a pillar and to engrave upon the side thereof this sentence: 'Over this stile is the way to Doubting Castle, which is kept by Giant Despair, who despiseth the King of the Celestial Country, and seeks to destroy His holy pilgrims.'[5]

This is wonderful writing. Christian already had in his possession his means of escape: a key represents divine promises of liberation.

Now, don't infer from this a trite, self-help moral, as if the cave-dweller's solution is merely to recall old truths. Bunyan's point for the despairing seems to be that our hope depends not on what we possess as such, but on the one who makes these promises: God himself. Giant Despair had completely obscured the pilgrims' view of him, the only one who ultimately makes hope possible in the first place. What relief it is to know that the God revealed in Christ is a God who specializes in promise making and promise keeping.

But this prompts an obvious, but fundamental, question. What *are* those promises for cave-dwellers? As should be clear by now, God never promised anyone a life free of stress, pain or complexity. But he did certainly promise to accompany us along the Way – after all, one of the most cherished names for God in the Bible is Immanuel, meaning 'God with us'. We are not alone. But, even more significantly, we are promised a welcome at the Way's end, the chance at last to cease from striving, to catch one's breath, above all, to REST. But this will not be a rest equivalent to dreamless or unrefreshing sleep. Instead, it will be restorative and healing. It will be what the Hebrew mind beautifully understood as *shalom*, whereby there is peace, integrity and integration, a repairing of all that was broken or shattered. This is the promise of the one who sits on heaven's throne:

> I saw the Holy City, the new Jerusalem, coming down out of heaven from God, prepared as a bride beautifully dressed for her husband. And I heard a loud voice from the throne saying, 'Look! God's dwelling-place is now among the people, and he will dwell with them. They will be his people, and God himself will be with them and be their God. "He will wipe every tear from their eyes. There will be no more death" or mourning or crying or pain, for the old order of things has passed away.'
>
> He who was seated on the throne said, 'I am making everything new!' Then he said, 'Write this down, for these words are trustworthy and true.'
> (Revelation 21:2–5)

## 9. THE GIFT

The elephant in the room throughout has been the 'M' word – ministry. Is pastoral ministry (in whatever form) possible for a cave-dweller?

From time to time, I have been asked this question by well-intentioned friends seeking positive, but realistic, advice. Should a church appoint someone with mental health challenges to their staff? Can sufferers realistically consider such work for themselves?

A generalized response is unwise, since answers must always be tailor-made to the individual and circumstances in view. Nevertheless, it is important to state that there is no intrinsic reason for it to be impossible. In fact, the reverse might be the case. I sometimes wonder, only half in jest, if it should almost be a job *requirement*.

Of course, there is a spectrum of mental health afflictions – and persistently extreme symptoms can make full-time employment of *any* kind problematic. But, for the most part, it is a question of good work–life patterns and coping mechanisms. In that respect, it is not so different from employing an amputee or someone allergic to gluten. Colleagues will inevitably need to make adjustments and allowances – just as should always be the case when appointing someone different from the team's majority culture.

That said, some ministries are probably less realistic than others. For example, overseas mission agencies tend to regard mental health issues as a bar to cross-cultural work, unless there are good grounds for doing otherwise. This is because living cross-culturally certainly compounds the stresses of modern living. It boils down to an individual's coping mechanisms and levels of resilience.

I did get to a point of no return, however, for a host of reasons. I could not figure out how to fit my job description in a relentlessly busy church around the limitations I gradually realized I had. Nobody forced me into it, by any means, but I just could not sustain the pace demanded by the job without significantly adding to the burdens of already busy colleagues. It could perhaps have been different if more aspects of my role had played better to my strengths and passions, but after nine years, I had changed, as had others. As is all too common, I returned from a combination of sabbatical and sick leave with the hope of making the best job of it, only to find that I couldn't.

So, reluctantly, I handed in my resignation, albeit with twelve months' notice to ensure an orderly handover. I also needed time to figure out what on earth we were going to do! Suddenly, we were stepping out into the unknown, after twenty years of ministry in UK and Uganda institutions. Rachel was very positive about the change, but we both needed time to identify the pieces of my work jigsaw, and then fit them together. In retrospect, having a whole year was probably too long for all concerned, but it is hard to know how we could have done it differently.

So, in a sense, my mental health challenges *were* a signifi-cant factor in stepping back from local church pastoral ministry. But depression did not cause me to 'leave ministry'. That couldn't be further from the truth. In fact, I was not leaving ministry at all; I was simply pastoring in ways that were (for me at least) new. Depression was a catalyst for changes in my ministry, but emphatically not an obstacle to my ministry. It was frustrating, to say the least, when a few asked me what I was going to do now that I was 'leaving ministry'.

So how might we understand the relationship between the pastor and the black dog?

## Meanings in the pain

It seems basic to being human. We crave meaning. This is not simply a question of significance in a vast universe. It is also the desire to be part of a story, one that can make sense of the turning points of our lives.

From time to time, I have entertained the delusional aspiration of being a novelist. It sounds like a nice idea, but I never got into creative writing at school, and I have fallen flat on my face on the few occasions when I attempted it. But I am fascinated by those who are good at it, and always curious to retrace their thought process when creating a character or plot. One thing is clear, however, in all but the most gifted writers (and even they need to be careful about this sometimes). Every detail or description must have significance in the storytelling. It can give a sense of place or atmosphere, perhaps (although overdoing this can be a litmus test for bad writing) – but it is vital to have reasons for it. As editors Sandra Newman and Howard Mittelmark put it:

The good news is that as a writer of fiction you get to create your world from scratch. The bad news is that because you create your world from scratch, everything in it is a conscious choice, and the reader will assume that there is some reason behind these choices . . .

For similar reasons, details that would go unremarked in real life – a quick glance across the room, the lyrics of the song that's playing when you enter a bar – take on much greater significance in fiction. If *you* have to run dripping from the shower to sign for an unexpected package, it is probably the gardening clogs you ordered from Lands' End. But if your character is interrupted in the shower by the arrival of an unexpected package, it tells your readers that the package will unleash a momentous chain of events.[1]

Life is just not neat. It's one of the things that makes truth stranger than fiction. In life, some things just 'are'. They are incidental, and have little immediate or obvious meaning. That is not to suggest they have no meaning for any-one, necessarily, just that they are irrelevant to our own lives.

But because we sense that our lives are part of a story – and in theological terms, they genuinely are, because we all get swept up into God's story – we expect to find meaning in everything. Unfortunately, it is not quite as simple as that. As we have already seen, there is still great mystery, even *after* clinging to the Christ-story that insists on God working all things together for the good.

For, in the vast majority of circumstances, suffering cannot be inherently good. So mental illness cannot be a good thing. It is one of many tragic features of a fallen creation that can only groan until it is redeemed and restored. I wouldn't wish it on my worst enemy. There is an irrationality to it – as there nearly always is with evil – an absurd pointlessness to its corrosive, energy-sapping pain. More than that, suffering far exceeds the capacities of human understanding. We simply cannot know what it is all about.

It is a very different matter to see how good might come from it. So, for example, it could be our body and soul's way of telling us that something in life is out of sync. We have been driving ourselves too hard, or trying to contain too much pain alone, or even simply forgetting we are human beings with finite physical, mental and spiritual resources. Mental illness is in this instance the canary in the mine, the internal alarm shouting at us to change direction. It serves an important, lifesaving purpose.

This is not generally the case for those with chronic mental health issues, however. For them, it may just be a fact of their reality, to which she or he must adjust. It might be a poisonous cocktail of genetic inheritance, painful memories, tough circumstances and possibly lifestyle choices. Or none of the above.

The question remains, however. Can any meaning be derived from this mental suffering?

### The divine precedent

The supreme precedent that has helped me here is Christ's cross. For, quite apart from the premeditated horrors of crucifixion as a means of tortured execution, in kingdom of God terms it was unequivocally humanity's worst act. It is as futile as it sounds – but at the cross, creatures killed their Creator. That was the logical end of the road, though, a trajectory that began with humanity's rejection of divine authority in Eden.

So what was the worst thing ever to take place on earth? The cross.

Yet the sight that comes from faith – in other words, the perspective shaped by what God has revealed and achieved – views things very differently. It looks beyond appearances to the substance. To the eyes of faith, the cross is a victory and an act of genius – the only place in human history where perfect justice has met with perfect mercy.

So what was the greatest event ever to take place on earth? The cross. As the poet and theologian Malcolm Guite beautifully phrased it, 'In a daring and beautiful creative reversal, God takes the worst we can do to him and turns it into the very best that He can do for us.'[2]

Peter grappled with precisely this point when he preached at Pentecost:

> This man was handed over to you by God's deliberate plan and foreknowledge; and you, with the help of wicked men, put him to death by nailing him to the cross. But God raised him from the dead, freeing him from the agony of death, because it was impossible for death to keep its hold on him.
> (Acts 2:23–24)

This is the kind of statement that makes the brain hurt. It is impossible to understand it fully. In many ways, it tries to have its theological cake and eat it. Peter insists that God is in control – the cross was always integral to his plan (from Genesis 3:15 onwards, and even before creation, according to Revelation 13:8). But human beings are simultaneously responsible; we are not programmed automata without accountability, creativity or rationality. The cross was a human act of brutal execution – the result of an unholy alliance between Roman imperialists and Jewish opportunists and radicals. So the cross was the darkest human act; it was also the pre-eminent divine act.

This must be the deepest mystery in the gospel story. My purpose in mentioning it is not to perplex, far less to annoy. It is simply to suggest that it offers a model for how we might see suffering in a different light. It is not directly analogous, because the cross is a supremely redemptive act, whereas mental illness is not (at least, not in the same way). So we should steer clear from suggesting that the good God directly causes evil. Instead, we know that, in his goodness, he redeems and overcomes it. In fact, his redemptive act obliterates the evil to such an extent that it is as if the whole thing (in retrospect) has become 'a good'.

It is what Tolkien called a 'eucatastrophe' – a sudden turn of events that changes everything for the better, at precisely the moment when all seemed lost. Thus, at the climax of the *Lord of the Rings* trilogy, on a precipice overlooking the churning fires of Mount Doom, Frodo has one final fight with Gollum for the Ring. The fate of Middle Earth is instantly transformed when Gollum seizes his prize only to find himself falling headlong into the furnace. But Tolkien regarded the greatest eucatastrophe of them all to be Christ's resurrection after the tragedy of Good Friday. All looked lost – until that Easter Sunday. That changed everything.

This explains why the apostle Paul could make statements like this, I suspect: 'I consider that our present sufferings are not worth comparing with the glory that will be revealed in us' (Romans 8:18). In no sense is he making light of the sufferings – no-one with a pastoral heart could conceive of doing that. He is simply giving the promised glory its due weight.

### The divine gift
Now, if that suffering, and our perspective on it, can help others to reach the confidence of Romans 8:18, then I think

it can be said to have meaning. This is where I think pastoral ministry has a part to play.

For, just as it is a blessed relief to encounter other cave-dwellers, it changes everything to know that our own experience of pain can help someone else's. It is, in that sense, redemptive. Despite what some suggest, it is nearly always inappropriate to utter the words 'I know how you feel', at least without deep exploration and conversation. It is too glib, too dismissive. But if sharing my own story leads someone to recognize that he or she is not the only one, or the first, or the worst – in other words, if my story resonates in some way with another's – then I am profoundly moved to gratitude and hope. I can see that God does have some sort of purpose in it all, that I can be used to help others along the Way. Dare I say it, I can actually begin to see this whole saga as a divine gift.

That will seem absurd. And at one level it is. I can *never* say that I'm glad to battle with depression. I loathe it with a passion. I hate the way I can so easily get derailed or befuddled. I detest the way my issues adversely affect my wife, family and close friends. NONE of that is a gift.

Yet there is something consistent here with how God so often does 'the gifts thing'. In contrast to the way many naturally think, God rarely grants a gift for the benefit of its recipient. That is a classically Western mistake because it is shaped by our obsessive individualism. To be fair, though, if I give my wife a birthday present, it is not unreasonable of her to assume that it really is for her. Which is why she was a little miffed once to receive a CD of music that I liked more than she did! But, as Paul wrote to the Corinthians in his famous section on spiritual gifts, 'to each one the manifestation of the Spirit is given for the common good' (1 Corinthians 12:7). In other words, in the Christian family, each of us is given gifts in order to serve others. This is why Paul launches into that sublimely challenging, but oft misunderstood, reflection on how love works in the very next chapter (1 Corinthians 13). The gifts we each have are designed to help us love others in our own unique way.

So, if my experiences as a cave-dweller help me to 'carry each other's burdens, and in this way [to] fulfil the law of Christ' (Galatians 6:2), then I can genuinely see them as a gift. I do not need to identify a divine causal link to my depression to sense a divine purpose in it. My tears now have redemptive meaning. Paul seems to have alluded to his own experience of precisely this process in his second Corinthian letter. Because God comforts us in our troubles, 'we can comfort those in any trouble with the comfort we ourselves receive from God' (2 Corinthian 1:4).

Consequently, I have come to believe that my depression has made me a better pastor.

### The divine purpose

We should not imagine that this 'gift' is without its bene-fits. We are assured by several New Testament writers that God can and does use our sufferings (whatever their causes) for our good:

- Peter writes, at the start of his first letter, that the grief his readers have suffered 'in all kinds of trials' has a refining effect, purifying a believer's faith, which has 'greater worth than gold' (1 Peter 1:6–7).
- The writer to the Hebrews can also state that there is discipline to our suffering, and that, when done properly, a father will only discipline out of love. Because he loves us, and therefore wants the best for us, God works through our sufferings so that we might 'share in his holiness' (Hebrews 12:6, 10–11).

- Paul has much to teach about suffering – but one of his most startling comments must surely be his conviction about knowing Christ. This means that he will 'know the power of his resurrection and participation in his sufferings, becoming like him in his death, and so, somehow, attaining to the resurrection from the dead' (Philippians 3:10–11).

I can understand wanting a taste of Christ's resurrection – but his sufferings? Not so much! But whatever the world and life throw at us, we can know that he truly has blazed the trail ahead of us. We share in what he endured – he identifies with every aspect of the cave experience. This is the grounds of our hope. For, because of him, we know it will not last indefinitely, and, even more importantly, he can uniquely say, 'I know how you feel.'

In summary, God is working for our good, through every experience and circumstance of our lives. There *is* a story being written in our lives that gives the details some significance. The good that he works for us through everything is not what we instinctively wish for, but is for our benefit (Romans 8:28). For the highest good I can receive is my greatest conformity to Christ himself. This is his ultimate purpose for each one of us: 'Therefore we do not lose heart. Though outwardly we are wasting away, yet inwardly we are being renewed day by day. For our light and momentary troubles are achieving for us an eternal glory that far outweighs them all' (2 Corinthians 4:16–17). It is simply that it takes the eye of faith, not sight, to believe this.

To be honest, I have struggled with what all three of these biblical writers say. I recoil from it – because in the darkness of the cave, it seems so cruel and malicious. Is it *really* that necessary?

A dear friend was diagnosed with breast cancer late last year. She's not yet forty and has young children. She and her husband have been remarkable in how they have handled the whole process – Rachel and I have learned a great deal from them in this. She has courageously submitted to the medical marathon of chemotherapy over several months, then daily radiotherapy for a few weeks, and then some aggressive wonder drugs. It has been a miserable experience. The *only* reason anyone would willingly surrender to it all is the potential good that can come from it. Thankfully, our friend's chances of a recurrence are now almost equivalent to those of someone who had never had a tumour in the first place.

Twelve years of cave dwelling, albeit at varying depths and intensities, have left me wondering, nevertheless. That is quite the endurance test. I have no idea how much longer it will continue. I didn't have a surgeon prepare me in advance – explaining what lay ahead and how it might contribute to my refinement. I didn't have someone help my family adjust to a cave-dwelling husband or dad – especially when he seems to be tearing his own hair out rather than having chemicals do the trick. That would have made it easier, I suppose. But I do have the apostles, each pointing me to trust in a providential hand at work, turning everything I go through for my eternal good.

It's just that I must take that on faith. Even on the better days. Because it sure doesn't feel like it's making me a better person at times! But, because I do take God's word for it, I trust that the value of these times *will* become clear one day. As Zack Eswine rather wonderfully puts it, 'We must learn how to live when only God knows what is going on truly or completely.'[3] After all, can anyone else *ever* be said genuinely to know what is going on?

## Ministry through our weakness

I never expected to reflect as deeply on the nature of ministry as I have done. I'm sure I would never have done so without the black dog's provocations. But I have realized that there are aspects that should shape and form pastoral work for us all, regardless of our mental health.

I heard this story a while back and it has had a profound effect on me since:

> John, the senior pastor of a small church in Ireland, was joined by a new assistant. We'll call him Charlie. So, early on in Charlie's time, John would take him on pastoral visits, for funerals and weddings and all the rest – just so he could learn the ropes. It was all pretty normal.
>
> One day they were going to visit Fred, a church member who had seriously messed up his life. Just about everything that could go wrong had gone wrong. His business had collapsed, his family was breaking up, and now the police were involved.
>
> And you know what the worst thing was? It was all the consequence of his own folly.
>
> As they walked along, the senior man asked his assistant, 'Could you see yourself ever getting into the sort of mess Fred is in?'
>
> Charlie was quiet for a moment. Eventually he replied, 'It's just terrible, isn't it? My heart goes out to him – and to the family. I just can't imagine it and really wouldn't wish this on my worst enemy. But I guess the terrible truth in the end is that he only has himself to blame . . . So, no, I don't think so.'
>
> 'Well, in that case,' said John gently but emphatically, 'I think it's best if you go home and I'll go on alone.'

I have known pastors like Charlie, but, thankfully, have known others like John. There's no contest over who I want alongside me in a crisis.

Good pastors are not perfect pastors. No pastor is a perfect pastor. Good pastors are, paradoxically, those who know their own limitations, their imperfections. We give lip-service to this truth. But it is, sadly, rare to encounter leaders who know their own limitations and imperfections, and intentionally gather around them others who can complement those limitations and compensate for their shortcomings. It is rare to find leaders who are weak, but then are strong enough to admit it.

### The necessity of weakness

The apostle Paul was one such. This explains his bizarre argument at the end of 2 Corinthians. Corinth, that notorious double-port city, was a boisterous, cosmopolitan and showy place, on the up. People there tended only to be impressed by the spectacular or astonishing. If Paul had wanted to play that game, he could easily have gloried at length in his own unique spiritual journey. He coyly refers to himself as 'a man in Christ' (12:2) who did indeed have some weird experiences. But he resists that, because his boast is subversively different. He boasts in his weakness (12:5).

He knows that his spiritual encounters (what he calls 'these surpassingly great revelations', 12:7) could have had a detrimental effect:

> Therefore, in order to keep me from becoming conceited,
> I was given a thorn in my flesh, a messenger of Satan, to
> torment me. Three times I pleaded with the Lord to take
> it away from me. But he said to me, 'My grace is sufficient
> for you, for my power is made perfect in weakness.' Therefore

I will boast all the more gladly about my weaknesses, so that
Christ's power may rest on me. That is why, for Christ's sake,
I delight in weaknesses, in insults, in hardships, in persecutions,
in difficulties. For when I am weak, then I am strong.
(2 Corinthians 12:7–10)

It is irrelevant what Paul's thorn was precisely. Countless
interpreters have made their guesses, some educated, some
less so. It is likely to have been a physical ailment of some sort,
but who knows? What stuns me every time was his willingness
to stop praying for its removal after only three times! I have
lost count of the number of times I've prayed about my own
'thorn'. I must confess a struggle to being content with the
Lord's strength in the face of my weakness.

But I have learned this. The people who scare me most are
the leaders who admit no weakness. They are either living in
a super-spiritual fog without self-awareness . . . or they wish
they could admit it, but are too scared of the repercussions
in over-critical and graceless church cultures, and so, perhaps,
over-compensate by polishing the façade of 'sortedness' . . .
or they are plain old hypocrites.

As someone once put it, never trust a leader without a limp.
How else can any of us be brought to the end of ourselves
enough to be forced to throw ourselves on God's mercy?
We're all too proud and independent to do that by nature. But
a limp is hard to hide – and, in fact, does not need to be
hidden.

The image originates in that strange, perplexing story of
Jacob wrestling with God, in Genesis 32. It is one of the Bible's
great turning points, resulting in this wily and rather un-
pleasant character being utterly transformed. Thereafter,
Jacob (which means 'deceiver') is granted the name Israel
(which means 'wrestled with God') because he has 'struggled

with God and with humans and [has] overcome' (Genesis 32:28). It is deeply mysterious and hard to imagine. At the very least, it means he persisted in clinging to God, however hard that became. But, during the wrestling match, he was wounded in such a way that he would never forget that night's events. With seemingly the lightest of divine touches, God for ever damaged his hip socket.

The importance is simple – leaders who limp are those who are weak and know it, but are not threatened by it. They have no alternative *but* to trust God. They know they cannot manage on their own; they simply don't have it in them. And yet, still they lead, and even thrive. For that, only God can take credit. That is how it was always meant to be for anyone in Christian ministry.

I can't be sure of this, but I suspect that what Paul says about weakness here is all-inclusive:

- It is undoubtedly physical weakness – we are all limited in every way. Nothing about us is infinite: each of us gets sick; most of us will get old; and all of us will die.
- It is also emotional weakness – each of us has a limited capacity for others and their needs (whether we are in pastoral ministry or not). There are days when we simply can't take any more. We all bear the scars of ministry griefs and pains.
- But it must surely also include spiritual weakness – we have limits for fighting temptations; we become prayerless; we get fearful and anxious, unable (or even unwilling) to trust in God's good purposes. We struggle to live by faith because we would far prefer to live by sight.

All of this is evidence of our flaws.

But how often do our church cultures reflect that reality? We present a good front; we wear the respectability mask, which shows that all is fine, especially in middle-class, professional contexts. We have perfected the art of looking good. And I'm not just referring to the church staff team. This is very Corinthian. And it is the shortcut to spiritual despair or pervasive hypocrisy, or both.

But Paul subverts both – simply by being upfront. He is unashamed of his weakness. Why? It is because his strength, as well as his identity and purpose, all derive from the security he has discovered in Christ. Christ brings the forgiveness for his guilt, the acceptance that heals his shame, the strength that assuages his insecurities. Paul does not derive his sense of worth, nor understand his identity, from either his role in ministry, or from afflictions and weakness. In short, the thorn keeps him humble, while God's grace frees him from pretence.

The issue is whether or not we are willing to do that openly and honestly. This is not a call to hang out all the dirty washing for all to see. There is no need for every detail to be public – though it is important for a *handful* to know (for the sake of our accountability). Public information needs to be limited, especially where it impinges on the privacy of others. What matters is a public acknowledgment of the *fact* of one's flaws and limitations (which are obvious to people anyway). If I can put it starkly, we should learn to do weakness and failure well.

This takes care and thought, since there are no easy shortcuts. It is a combination of direction from the front, and a community's willingness to participate in extending real grace and acceptance. Very often, people will only be willing to extend grace to others in trouble if they have experienced grace themselves. There is a catch-22 situation here. For leaders to be willing to share their struggles publicly, there needs to be a church culture that makes that safe. But making it safe requires leadership and the sharing of grace. That is demanding and risky. But nobody ever said the best way to live together was the easiest way to live together.

So here are a few indicators that we would all do well to consider carefully:

- How often do we admit to having doubts or questions? Admit to struggling to understand something? To being out of our depth?
- How quickly to do we lean on the Lord? Not just publicly, but privately in prayer with friends and others, over things that are difficult or overwhelming?
- How readily do we seek help?
- How do we cope when others around us are better at something than we are? Are we threatened by them or do we gratefully encourage them?

In short, how well do we do at pastoring out of the reality of our own limitations? Or is our ministry a way of covering them up? If we can't get this right, then there's little chance that the congregation will, since, for better or for worse, a church's subculture is set by a church's leadership.

### The trajectory of shalom

Paul's so-called pastoral letters, those written to individuals rather than church congregations, show a warmth that surprises many. They also show how realistic and down to earth he was. Thus, when he writes to Timothy – a man with whom he had worked for years and known for even longer – he clearly does so with great affection. After giving important instructions for his next ministry, he says, 'Be diligent in these matters; give yourself wholly to them, so that everyone may see your progress' (1 Timothy 4:15).

I love that verse for its last word. Progress. Paul doesn't ask for the moon – just forward momentum. Because our lives are a pilgrimage, each of us walks at our own pace in our own unique way to our common destination: being with Christ himself. What matters for leaders is not so much our progress along the Way, but the fact that people can see it. In other words, it is possible to tell how far we have already come in the time that we have been with them. This serves to encourage them to walk it as well, and to learn how they can perhaps do it better. Or at least to learn from our mistakes.

But what of that destination? What will it be like on that day when we are united with Christ? More to the point, what will *we* be like? To grasp this, let us return to what we have only touched on thus far: *shalom*.

*Shalom* is a diamond word – its sparkling beauty is complex and impossible to reduce or summarize in one word alone. It has too many facets. The common English translation of 'peace' – as when Jeremiah's contemporaries proclaim, '*Shalom, shalom*, when there is no *shalom*' (Jeremiah 6:14) – goes nowhere close to capturing those facets. Its roots give a sense of being 'whole' or 'undivided' – which is why it can have the connotations of good health and well-being. Consequently, this peace is far greater than the mere absence of war, although it is clearly at least that.

*Shalom* is about the restoration and renewal of everything that was damaged or destroyed in the course of that war. That includes every broken relationship. Thus, *shalom* also means social harmony, with all relating well and openly, honestly and truthfully. This, ultimately, is a community in which no masks are worn because no masks are necessary. This is because each member of that community has known the joy of wounds bound and scars healed, broken hearts mended and tears wiped away. The anger and resentments that divide us have been overcome. *Shalom* overcomes the brokenness of Western individualism, since when God promises *shalom*, it is invariably plural:

'I have seen their ways, but I will heal them;
   I will guide them and restore comfort to Israel's
      mourners,
   creating praise on their lips.
Peace, peace, to those far and near,'
   says the LORD. 'And I will heal them.'
(Isaiah 57:18–19)

Yet, for me, the most anticipated ingredient of *shalom* healing is inevitably the psychological.

I have never forgotten Pat. She was a stalwart member of the first church I ever worked for in Oxford. I was just a junior member of the team, in a role that perfectly suited me at the time – a few ministry responsibilities, plus general dogsbody jobs around the site and congregation. It did mean that I got to know the wider congregation whom otherwise I wouldn't have met. I forget the precise diagnosis, but Pat suffered from a crippling, degenerative bone disease – her skeleton seemed to be simultaneously fusing and fragmenting. She was encased in various splints, but had what was then a state-of-the-art motorized buggy, so it seemed that nothing could hold her back. She would hurtle along Oxford pavements so that she never missed times of fellowship. I only heard from others that she was in permanent pain – but she would always talk about her hope. And the closest thing to a complaint that I ever heard from her was, 'Mark, I can't wait for my resurrection body!' Sadly, we did not keep in touch, and she died just a few years after I moved on. But I imagine her at last enjoying what she so faithfully anticipated.

Well, I probably do whinge and complain too much. To that extent, I have not followed her lead very well. But I will never forget the vibrancy of her expectant hope. And, in my better moments, I do echo that in my heart and prayers. I am looking forward to my resurrection body; but I am looking forward to my resurrection mind and soul even more. Because then, God's heavenly *shalom* will obliterate the blizzard for ever, my perspectives will be clear, and my love for others unsullied.

But what has this to do with ministry?

If our trajectory is heading towards perfect peace with Christ, towards knowing his completed work in us, then ministry is to prepare people for that point. Of course, it includes bringing people to a point of *wanting* to be with Christ – it is hard to do without that element. But it is also a matter of helping people grow in their faith and persevere on the Way – so that their lives reflect that objective ever more faithfully. This is how Paul explained his work: '[Christ] is the one we proclaim, admonishing and teaching everyone with all wisdom, so that we may present everyone fully mature in Christ. To this end I strenuously contend with all the energy Christ so powerfully works in me' (Colossians 1:28–29).

The goal is for all to be 'fully mature' – the King James Version translated it as 'perfect'. A literal translation might be 'complete'. It all comes to the same thing. Even though 'present everyone in *shalom*' would not qualify as an accurate translation, it does tally with Paul's point. It is about everything coming together in someone's life in its right place. That can only come about through Christ. In this life, our purpose is to grow towards that, and ministry is to encourage that. If Christ's *shalom* is the goal of the Way, then it stands to reason that the journey to get there must be characterized by *shalom*.

In other words, we are seeking to live and serve in such a way that brings others to their full flourishing and integration in Christ. The task will never be complete in this life. Indeed, the task *can* never be complete in this life. But that is no excuse for passivity. That is why ministry is a matter for strenuous effort, with 'all the energy Christ so powerfully works in me'. But the paradox is that it requires an acceptance of our weakness to lean on God for his strength.

If the acknowledgment of my own brokenness can somehow contribute to another person's reintegration, to inspire their clinging while beset by darkness or fog or blizzards, to offer help for the next few steps along the Way, simply because I am just a few steps ahead, then I count it as nothing less than a privilege. I know how much I have needed others like that over the years. To be able to pass on the compliment changes everything. It is for that reason that I have begun to see these afflictions, this unremoved thorn, as a severe mercy, and, even, a divine gift.

## APPENDIX 1: MANAGING THE SYMPTOMS

Here are some very brief pointers and practical lessons learnt along the Way. Because ministry is relentless – there is *always* another need, another demand, another opportunity, another crisis – and we are finite and broken, we must take care. We are not superheroes. And cave-dwellers in ministry must find a rhythm that keeps them functioning well. I need to learn to live, and minister, with and through the person that I am – with the gifts God has given me, despite the flaws that I indulge, with the weaknesses I have discovered, and the environments in which I thrive.

### Know yourself

At the spectacular mountain shrine to the god Apollo at Delphi in ancient Greece, various inscriptions greeted visiting worshippers. The two most famous were 'nothing in excess' and 'know yourself'. Those simple phrases contain great wisdom, and the latter is especially important for the cave-dweller. It will take time to understand ourselves (some characteristics have taken me at least a decade to identify), which is why there will be bumps and bruises along the Way. But here are some of the discoveries we need if we are to manage our symptoms:

- **Triggers**: are there specific situations or contexts (or even discussion topics) that provoke anxiety or other strong emotions that are out of proportion to the trigger itself? Are these manageable, or can they be avoided altogether?
- **Techniques**: are there ways of talking yourself down from those emotions, or to alleviate any physical symptoms (like breathing exercises)? Is there a thought process you can repeat in your mind to help regain perspective?
- **Resilience**: are there ways of developing greater resilience for your defences, so that old triggers bother you less? There are many resources online if you lack local support for this. A therapist can help especially here.
- **Rest**: hobbies and pastimes, time off, retreats, escaping to favourite places – all of these are of fundamental importance to self-care and effective ministry for cave-dwellers. We all need to recharge batteries. All of us need a 'hinterland', aspects of life outside our work and daily routines. It doesn't matter what it is, as long as it is there.

## Get help

We are not created for isolation. We are meant to share burdens and tears. Please ensure that you have people around you. And if you don't seem to have any, then pray for some.

It may be that this is especially hard for those in ministry – because everyone looks up to them and expects them to be sorted. They go around helping everyone else and forget to pay attention to their own needs.

Jesus quoted a proverb that was doing the rounds in his day: 'Physician, heal yourself!' (Luke 4:23). In context, he was preaching to his home crowd in Nazareth, fully anticipating the scepticism of his former neighbours. He pre-empted their rejection of him by quoting this proverb. He expected their memories of his childhood, say, to inoculate them against listening to him in adulthood, and therefore to tell him to mind his own problems before talking about theirs. If there ever was a proverb that did apply to Jesus, this was it. But it has not dated for the rest of us. We too often ignore our own needs, in the absurd belief that self-care might somehow be worldly. After all, in the end, swallowing pride in order to ask for help is preferable to collapse and burn-out.

- **Friends**: have one or two individuals with whom you can talk safely about the darkest moments. If you are plagued by suicidal thoughts, it is crucial. Develop a set of shared code words, so that you can avoid stark or difficult words. This is also very helpful for close family members. Learn to trust them enough to establish the difference between real and not real.
- **Professionals**: there are many types of therapist and schools of thought. Sometimes it takes time to find someone you relate to well. It can take a few sessions before discovering whether or not you click – if you don't, move on. It's fine. But I have especially benefitted from two or three who helped me to find links and connections from different stages of my whole life. This has been crucial for finding coping mechanisms

with triggers. If you are in the UK, you can of course receive therapy on the NHS, through a referral from your GP.

- **God**: brief one-liner prayers, or even one-word prayers (like 'Help!'), are good. Even groans to God are acceptable – the Holy Spirit knows exactly how to handle those (Romans 8:23). There have been times when I couldn't even pray. But I have asked my closest friends to do so for me. And where I have lacked the words, I have found such balm in some of the great Anglican liturgies of the Book of Common Prayer (BCP), or prayer anthologies (such as Arthur Bennett's wonderful collection of Puritan prayers, *The Valley of Vision*[1]). I have very recently been given a wonderful collection of personal and family liturgies by Douglas McKelvey, called *Every Moment Holy*.[2] It is a rich blessing indeed. But my most regular solace comes from Cranmer's prayers of Evening Prayer and Compline in the BCP. They are wonderful for regaining a degree of perspective as the last thing before bed, because when I'm travelling, the toughest times often come later at night.

*A brief word about medication*

I have been taking medication ever since my PTSD diagnosis in 2005, with a bit of trial and error along the way with different prescriptions. Some made little difference; one or two made matters far worse, but the two that I've taken for the longest seem to help me preserve an equilibrium of sorts. I doubt I would have been able to work for a busy church for nine years without them. But, of course, it's impossible to know for sure.

A few years ago, I was suddenly freaked out by the pills. I unilaterally stopped taking them, without telling my doctor.

Foolish. I suffered quite a significant nosedive. Essentially, I had been overthinking, worrying that I had lost my identity, that this 'Mark Meynell person' didn't really exist, but somehow was the product of chemicals squished into tiny white tablets. Where was the real me? My state seemed so fake and artificial. I was just so confused.

I am all too aware of the debates about psychiatric medicine – and that the views of both health professionals and thoughtful Christians vary widely. It does perplex me how 'trial and error' drug prescription can feel. Yet I do know that medication helped me to retain some stability. It was never designed to cure. Instead, it enabled me to stand sufficiently still to make the most of therapy. And I have had a *lot* of therapy. I've lost count of the number of hours and approaches, let alone the cost. I saw one or two therapists who were total disasters, but two were great. One, whom I saw for three years, and another, for just under a year, have made a significant difference. Both helped to make connections between my earliest experiences and those more recently. Both reassured me that I hadn't gone mad – but that the convergence of events with my temperament and character would have made even the strongest crack.

The above is hardly an exhaustive list. It doesn't matter how you get help, though, just as long as you do. It might be hard to adjust to the reality that others cannot be fixers. We must resist expecting them to, just as we would expect our friends not to try to fix us.

## Serve others

Finally, it can be very encouraging and healing to be able to help others in pain. Your own afflictions should not be a long-term excuse to avoid loving and serving others. But it is vital to know your limits and to find ways to protect your own psychological equilibrium when with others. We cannot save the world; we cannot even save ourselves. So we will not be able to save other cave-dwellers. Our task may simply be to let them know we are fellow-travellers.

If this book has helped you in any way, then I am very glad. I know my own limits, though, and there is no way that I am going to be able to take on all the personal challenges of those who do read it (assuming that there will be more than a few!).

## APPENDIX 2: UNEXPECTED FRIENDS IN THE CAVE

This is inevitably, and unashamedly, a personal list, a reflection of my own walk along the Way. It's doubtful if every item will appeal to every reader. Hopefully, it will offer some ideas for where to make 'new friends'.

### Words for the cave

*Favourite reads*

It is perhaps surprising, but the books that have most helped me are those that are more specifically personal rather than those that are generic or prescriptive. This is probably because they never claim to be more than what they are – namely, a testimony or memoir. The books that I have struggled most with are those that rush to tell me what it's always like and what I should do. So this very selective list reflects that bias away from the more theological or pastoral (however competent or useful they might be in parts):

William Styron, *Darkness Visible: A Memoir of Madness* (Vintage, 1992). For me, nothing else compares. Written from a secular perspective, but with a novelist's flair for capturing the inexpressible. The first true friend in print.

Matthew Johnstone, *I Had a Black Dog* (Robinson, 2007); and *Living with a Black* Dog (Robinson, 2009). What better way to convey the inexpressible than by dispensing with words altogether? Matthew Johnstone is a graphic artist who takes Winston Churchill's metaphor literally to convey the range of experiences he has gone through. He's used the same method in other books subsequently, but these were his first – I return to them often, and lend them frequently.

Zack Eswine, *The Imperfect Pastor* (formerly *Sensing Jesus*) (Crossway, 2015); and *Spurgeon's Sorrows: Realistic Hope for Those Who Suffer from Depression* (Christian Focus, 2015). I was gripped by the first of these two books – and loved it so much that I rushed out and bought a copy for all my colleagues at All Souls! It is a heart-warming, real, but challenging corrective to so much that has dehumanized and professionalized Christian ministry in the West (and is even better in its revised version as *The Imperfect Pastor*).

But *Spurgeon's Sorrows* represented a sea change. Having worked through the unique and vast archive of the great Victorian preacher's sermons, Eswine produced a book that I longed for without knowing it. It is brief but profound – part-biography, part-testimony, part-theological reflection, part-pastoral manual, part-biblical reflection. It is for me the best theological book on depression I know.

*Honourable mentions*

Matt Haig, *Reasons to Stay Alive* (Canongate, 2015). I loved
    Haig's quirkily brilliant novel *The Humans*, but could
    never quite put my finger on why it resonated so much.
    Reading this book explained everything – the novel is
    a veiled exploration of mental illness, and this unpacks
    how it affected him and, more importantly, how he was
    saved from the brink of suicide. Superbly down to earth.

Rachel Kelly, *Black Rainbow: How Words Healed Me* (Yellow
    Kite, 2014). A deeply moving testimony of depression,
    and how poetry was crucial to emerging from it.

Jo Swinney, *Through the Dark Woods* (Monarch, 2006). The
    first Christian treatment of depression that I didn't want
    to throw across the room in frustration or rage! Jo has
    subsequently become a friend, and she narrates her
    story with great wisdom and courage.

*Poetry*

I have nothing like the breadth of Rachel Kelly's literature
knowledge (see above), but have found specific poems
especially helpful or inspiring:

George Herbert (1593–1633)
    'Love (III)'
    'Bitter-Sweet'
    'A Wreath'
William Cowper (1731–1800)
    'The Stricken Deer' (from *The Task*)
    'God Moves in a Mysterious Way'
    'Sometimes a Light Surprises'
Gerard Manley Hopkins (1844–89)
    'As Kingfishers Catch Fire'
    'God's Grandeur'

D. H. Lawrence (1885–1930)
  'Healing'
T. S. Eliot (1888–1965)
  'Little Gidding', from *The Four Quartets*
  (although I won't pretend to understand it all!)
C. S. Lewis (1898–1963)
  'Love's as Warm as Tears'
Stevie Smith (1902–71)
  'Not Waving but Drowning'
Patrick Kavanagh (1904–68)
  'From Failure Up'
W. H. Auden (1907–73)
  'Musée des Beaux Arts'
R. S. Thomas (1913–2000)
  'The Bright Field'
  'The Kingdom'
Anna Kamienska (1920–86)
  'Tell Me What's the Difference'
Maya Angelou (1928–2014)
  'Touched by an Angel'
Anon
  'The Plum'

**Playlists for the cave**

For those who are so inclined, I have added as many of these songs and compositions as are available to some Spotify playlists. These can be found by searching for my profile name, *Quaesitor*.

Everyone's taste, especially when it comes to music, is different, of course. I'm eternally grateful for having had a broad and long musical education: piano from the age of six or seven, choirs and orchestras from nine, in a band (of very negligible quality!) in my teens. So the following lists reflect all of this. The world of classical, and especially choral, music has been close to my musical centre of gravity throughout my life.

There is not the space, inevitably, to describe why they matter to me: some meet me at my lowest ebb, helping to express cave reality (without necessarily wallowing in it); some capture a glorious reality or inexpressible emotion that I can latch on to; while others offer glimpses of an almost heavenly perfection, a reminder of hope for the sublime.

I'll leave you to discern which has which effect!

### Classical friends
This is not exhaustive, especially because I restricted myself to a maximum of two per composer. Some express the darkness, or blizzard, in ways that words cannot approach; others shine light in ways that make hope possible; others are just sublime foretastes of heaven.

Thomas Tallis, *Spem in Alium* (c.1570), 40-part motet

Claudio Monteverdi, *Vespro della Beata Vergine* (1610)

Henry Purcell, 'Sound the Trumpet' (1678)

Henry Purcell, 'When I Am Laid in Earth', Dido's Lament from *Dido and Aeneas* (1689)

George Frideric Handel, 'Eternal Source of Light Divine' (1713), a somewhat idolatrous birthday ode for Queen Anne!

Johann Sebastian Bach, 'Mache dich, mein Herze, rein', bass aria, *St Matthew Passion* (1727)

Johann Sebastian Bach, *Italian Concerto*, BWV 971 (1735)

Wolfgang Amadeus Mozart, 'Soave sia il vento' from *Così fan Tutte*, K588 (1790)

Wolfgang Amadeus Mozart, 'Ach, ich fühl's' from
  *The Magic Flute*, K620 (1791)

Ludwig van Beethoven, 'Pathétique', Piano Sonata
  in C minor, Op. 13 (1798)

Ludwig van Beethoven, 'Pastorale' Piano Sonata in D,
  Op. 28 (1801)

Franz Schubert, *Winterreise*, especially XXIV, 'Der
  Leiermann' (1827)

Franz Schubert, Piano Sonata in B flat, D960 (1828),
  his last piano sonata

Modest P. Mussorgsky, *Boris Godunov* (1868–9), an opera
  in four acts

Johannes Brahms, Symphony No. 4 in E minor, Op. 98
  (1885)

Antonin Dvořák, Romantic Pieces for Violin and Piano,
  Op. 75 (1887), especially the first movement

Edward Elgar, *Serenade for Strings*, Op. 20 (1892)

Gustav Mahler, Symphony No. 2, *Resurrection Symphony*
  (1888–94)

Johannes Brahms, Clarinet Sonata in E flat, Op. 120 (1894)

Edward Elgar, *The Dream of Gerontius* (1900), despite its
  theology!

Ralph Vaughan Williams, *Five Mystical Songs* (1906–12)

Richard Strauss, *Four Last Songs*, TrV 296 (1912–15)

Jean Sibelius, third movement of Symphony No. 5 in E flat,
  Op. 82 (1915) (Strawberry Switchblade stole the theme
  in the 1980s, but only Sibelius knew what to do with it)

William Henry Harris, *Faire Is the Heaven* (1925), for
  unaccompanied double choir

Francis Poulenc, *Trois Novelettes* for piano (1927), evoking
  for me the idyllic laziness of French summer evenings

William Walton, *Belshazzar's Feast* for bass, double choir
  and orchestra (1931)

Francis Poulenc, Larghetto from Concerto for Two Pianos
and Orchestra (1932)

Sergei Prokofiev, 'The Battle on the Ice' and 'Alexander's
Entry' from *Alexander Nevsky* (1938)

Aaron Copland, *Quiet City* for orchestra (1940)

Marcel Dupré, *Évocation*, Op. 37 for organ (1941)

Dmitri Shostakovich, Symphony No. 8, Op. 65 (1942)

Herbert Howells, *Collegium Regale* (1944–56), canticles
and service setting

Benjamin Britten, 'Sea Interludes' from *Peter Grimes* (1945)

Gerald Finzi, *Lo, the Full Final Sacrifice* (1946), for choir and
organ

Maurice Duruflé, 'In Paradisum' from his *Requiem* (1947)

Sergei Prokofiev, Symphony No. 7, Op. 131 (1952)

Dmitri Shostakovich, second movement (andante) from
Piano Concerto No. 2, Op. 102 (1957)

Benjamin Britten, *War Requiem*, especially 'Dies irae' and
'Let us sleep now' (1962)

Herbert Howells, 'Take Him, Earth, for Cherishing' (1964)

Einojuharni Rautavaara, *Cantus Arcticus: Concerto for Birds
and Orchestra* (1972)

Arvo Pärt, *Cantus in Memoriam Benjamin Britten* (1977)

Arvo Pärt, *Passio Domini Nostri Jesu Christi secundum Joannem*
(1982), especially the last fifteen minutes (but only after
listening to the whole thing)

Steve Reich, *Different Trains*, for string quartet and tape
(1988)

James MacMillan, *Veni, Veni, Emmanuel*, concerto for
percussion and orchestra (1992)

Eric Whitacre, *When David Heard* (2 Samuel 18:33) (1999)

Eric Whitacre, *Lux Aurumque* (2000)

Ēriks Ešenvalds, *Passion and Resurrection* (2005), for soprano,
mixed choir and strings

*The music of U2*

This deserves a chapter all by itself. I have written extensively online, and in one or two places in print, on why U2 matters (to me at least). It shocks some when I say it, but I do it without exaggeration, because I can testify to the fact that U2 has been instrumental in keeping my faltering Christian faith alive. Bono, in particular, is a poet, not a preacher, primarily, which is why some of his outpourings are ambiguous, opaque or downright perplexing. But that's fine.

What I admire him for is a relentless creative honesty that refuses to accept platitude or soundbite faith. That keeps us honest, if we have ears to hear – because he is always trying to figure out how on earth to hold to the old, old story in the chaos and darkness of now. I might not always like his answer – but I love that he helps me ask the question. He has the relentless faith in God to do that. That opens up space for me to do the same, even in the darkest recesses of the cave.

So, for what it's worth, here are my Top U2 Cave Songs (though I could have listed fifty without a sweat). They resonate at various phases of cave life – on the way in, in the pit, or as the fog lifts.

'40' (from *War*, 1983)
'Bad' (from *The Unforgettable Fire*, 1984) – especially live
'I Still Haven't Found What I'm Looking For' (from *The Joshua Tree*, 1987)
'Wave of Sorrow (Birdland)' (from *The Joshua Tree*, deluxe remastered edition, 1987)
'Love Rescue Me' (from *Rattle and Hum*, 1988)
'Ultraviolet (Light My Way)' (from *Achtung Baby*, 1991)
'Who's Gonna Ride Your Wild Horses' (from *Achtung Baby*, 1991)
'The First Time' (from *Zooropa*, 1993)

'Miss Sarajevo' (from *Passengers: Original Soundtracks 1*,
    1995)
'If God Will Send His Angels' (from *Pop*, 1997)
'Wake Up Dead Man' (from *Pop*, 1997)
'Beautiful Day' (from *All That You Can't Leave Behind*, 2000)
'Stuck in a Moment You Can't Get Out Of' (from *All That
    You Can't Leave Behind*, 2000)
'Walk On' (from *All That You Can't Leave Behind*, 2000)
'City of Blinding Lights' (from *How to Dismantle an Atomic
    Bomb*, 2004)
'Sometimes You Can't Make It on Your Own' (from *How
    to Dismantle an Atomic Bomb*, 2004)
'Yahweh' (from *How to Dismantle an Atomic Bomb*, 2004)
'Magnificent' (from *No Line on the Horizon*, 2009)
'Moment of Surrender' (from *No Line on the Horizon*, 2009)
'Unknown Caller' (from *No Line on the Horizon*, 2009)
'Every Breaking Wave' (from *Songs of Innocence*, 2014)

### Christian music

I do not listen to a great deal of so-called modern Christian
music. I'm being grossly unfair, but much of it seems too
trite, remote or simplistic – the kind of vinegary songs sung
to a heavy heart. However, these three albums are remarkable
exceptions. Each is the result of personal pain or tragedy –
which is certainly what gives them depth. All three have
proved to be reliable friends for protracted times in the cave.

Andrew Peterson, *The Burning Edge of Dawn* (Centricity
    Music, 2015). I have already quoted in full one standout
    song from this album: 'The Rain Keeps Falling'. It is
    uncanny, but, as mentioned, this one somehow managed
    to capture the totality of my cave experience. It is almost
    *too* painful to listen to, but it is truly cathartic – no other

song has ever reassured me as fully as this that I am not completely alone. But the whole album helps me cling to hope. Somehow.

Steve Curtis Chapman, *Beauty Will Rise* (Sparrow Records, 2009)

Nathan Tasker, *Man on a Wire* (Luxtone Records, 2014)

These two albums were both written at times of tragic bereavement – and they are raw but real. They model how to keep on living by faith instead of sight, especially when the blizzard feels at its most violent.

Of the many that have been recommended to me by fellow cave-dwellers, one other stands head and shoulders above the others: Gungor <www.gungormusic.com>. A band formed around the husband-and-wife team of Michael and Lisa Gungor has produced consistently interesting and edgy work. Many songs explore the realities and depths of human experience while all the time holding to God. Sometimes theological heterodox, occasionally eccentric and just plain odd, but, invariably, true balm for the soul.

 I have created some public Spotify playlists based on these lists, which you can find under my username Quaesitor, or by following the QR code.

## Online support for the cave

Mind and Soul <www.mindandsoul.info>
A British Christian site helping to think through the pain, the challenges and the needs of those with mental health issues from a faith perspective. As well as helpful resources to explore, this also provides a unique directory of British therapists (searchable by location and expertise).

The Mighty <themighty.com/mental-illness-list>
A vast global network of crowd-sourced articles and
testimonies covering all manner of afflictions. It does not
exclusively cover mental illness, but, if you have battles, it
would be very surprising not to find something to relate to!

Rethink Mental Illness <www.rethink.org>
General advice and wisdom from a secular perspective.

BCUK <www.biblicalcounselling.org.uk>
Christ-centred change, enabled by the Spirit, through the
ministry of the Word, in the local church.

CCEF <www.ccef.org/resources>
Christian Counselling and Education Foundation is a ministry
based in Pennsylvania, USA that offers excellent training,
counselling and resources in many countries, including in
the UK.

Metanoia <www.metanoia.org/suicide>
If you are feeling suicidal, then stop for a moment to read this
page. It's important.

ThinkTwice <thinktwiceinfo.org>
ThinkTwice aims to increase awareness and decrease
stigma so that people are as able to be open about their
mental health condition as they are about having the 'flu.
They provide training courses, consultancy, speakers and
writers.

There are numerous blogs out there, so this is hardly
exhaustive. But here are a number excellent ones that I have
found helpful from time to time (in no particular order):

Thorns and Gold (Tanya Marlow) <tanyamarlow.com>
Police Commander (John Sutherland) <policecommander.
   wordpress.com>
A New Name (Emma Scrivener) <emmascrivener.net>
Believer's Brain (Emma) <believersbrain.com>
Matt Bays, author, speaker <mattbayswriter.com>
The Long Walk Home (Kath Cunningham)
   <thelongwalkhome.co.uk>

## APPENDIX 3: SOME WORDS FROM INSIDE THE CAVE

This feels like the biggest risk of the book! If it's not your bag, or if you don't think these poems are up to much, then that's fine. I won't be offended. I certainly don't have great literary pretensions. But one or two friends in the cave have found that they resonate with them, not so much as great verse, but as an articulation of what they experience.

So, if they are helpful, excellent. If not, ignore. If they spur you to write your own, even better.

**Dread**
*On hearing Brahms' Fourth Symphony in a new light*

Acid reflux:
Caustic, corrosive,
Ruthless, regressive,
All hope, all kindness
Gnawed.

Flights delayed:
Pending, punishing
Stifling, stagnating
All joy, all laughter
Mute.

A passacaglia:
Rhythmic, relentless,
Seeping, seditious.
All life, all vigour
Sapped.

O Love, may this dread be forever consumed.
O Light, may your embers even feebly glow
O Lord, may my faith be never confounded.

## Shrugged Out

Words and deeds are barely
  symmetrical.
It's not that I ever thought
  they were;
it's just that I expected
  something
more parallel.

Bones by words are seldom
  fractured
except perhaps when others
  enact them.
But hearts by words quite
  often get broken
carelessly.

Whereas hearts by words can
  sure be stayed,
relieved, assured, retrieved,
  embraced.
But please! Don't presume that
  text and talk
are ample.

Because words and no deeds
  in fact are worse
Than deeds that spike and snag
  and shard
Because they seemed so sure,
  so true, so fond
But they're not.

They promised much,
  delivered little;
Unless by acts that buttressed
  sense
that showed a willing slant
  to bother
Unprompted.

So left, in cell, I felt, in doubt
with self, no guess, at fault,
  no doubt.
They tried, they thought, but
  crashed, and shrugged.
And left.

Yet when I suggested what
  seemed needed,
I wrestled to grasp why this,
  not heeded,
Could not be what was tried,
  persisted
despite me.

*Between Budapest and Heathrow*
*February 2016*

## Transfusion
*For Kosta*

I'm told my blood type's
 rare
naturally it's genetic, but it's
 the perfect curse
(as my grandmother might
 say)
– though they keep telling
 me it's 'a gift'.

Well in a way. But not
 to me.
I'm pleased to offer it,
 don't get me wrong.
But as with all God's gifts,
 it comes not for me,
 just through me.
There aren't exactly reciprocal
 benefits for universal
 donors.

Apart from the satisfaction
 of donating
that *is* good. It's much more
 blessed he said
And that I get. To see it's
 helped,
to hear a flagging heart
 revived. A joy. I mean it.

But. Here's the catch.

When *my* heart flags . . . and
 *I* need blood . . . what then
It's simply not the same for me
 as them
Perhaps I'm fussy; or prickly;
 or over-sensitive?
Yes I've had that told me more
 than once.

But doesn't that miss the point?
We choose our friends and not
 our genes
yet loyal friends whose pulse
 just doesn't match
by transfusion might sap or
 harm or even kill

They mean well; their
 intentions generous.
But when I need reviving,
 I need the same.
Compatibility I crave. It's all
 too rare.
Since universal donors aren't
 gifted universally.

So thank God, I'm not the only
 one . . .

*Vienna, April 2016*

## The Torment of Helios
*On seeing Paul Klee's* Sunset *(1930) at the Art Institute of Chicago*
*in April 2016*

In stately progress over horizons from east to west,
Helios knows
the shores that host the clans that spar
to oust and settle, seize and trample
for gain, for glory, for increase, for plenty.
yes, he knows.
While silently he glides across the lands, from dawns to dawns
he hears
the cries of cruelty and casualty from those who persist, old man,
in bleeding dry the countless dots that stop forever,
cries unheeded by the relentless music of the spheres.
But he hears.

With blistering blazing unblinking gaze across the nations
he sees,
with light he glares, exposing darkness deeds in every day,
mixed blessings for culprits, but victims too,
since light and life are clearly blessings, yet constrained
by perils and dangers of coming nights,
and impotent before persistent wrongs.
Yet he sees.

That Helian vantage must torment:
no wonder then the silent ache
from sound and sight of human wrong
no wonder then the frozen rage of
one
solitary
tear.

## The Nature of Tears

Come prickling tears, please
    stream your healing balm
Why maintain such cruel,
    strange reticence?

For lightest steps with ease
    the pheasants rouse
And provoke their strangled
    squawking bleats
to flight from fright of
    harmless threats

Or degreened leaves that slip
    when zephyred breezes
Flow with lightest caress or
    gentlest strokes
To gloriously paint the earth
    with nature's cloaks

Or shafts, by billows obscured,
    so quick return when winds
    are up;
With such silent slender ease
    they warm past clouds
'Til obscured again by El
    Greco's gilded shrouds

Or percussive home a
    woodpecker struck
With harmless head-butts the
    tree it beats
To forge a refuge with most
    casual techniques

So why, my prickling tears,
    refuse to shed?
Perhaps, it's pride, for blushes
    spared?
Or shame, for fear of weakness
    viewed?
Or even strength, so, needless
    seem?

But no, it's a heart by frost
    unseasonable
Gripped, still shaded with
    long-hid shadows.
Others warmed by shafts can
    laugh,
While mine still shivers in its
    hollowed home.
With practised masks and
    bonhomie
Are my tears pent up
but frozen.

*Ammerdown, Somerset*
*October 2016*

# A SMALL CLOSING WORD OF CAUTION

Of the handful of books that I've written, this was both the easiest and toughest by far. It was easiest in that it seemed to flow with very little effort – it almost felt as if it was just sitting there, waiting to emerge! Paradoxically, it was also the toughest, especially when it came to rereading and reviewing. You mean, I actually wrote/revealed/confessed *that*?

Inevitably, I fear the responses to it, as anyone who writes a book must (simply because once the words are out there, they take on a life of their own). It is an inherently exposing medium – and for all the appearance of expertise that writing a book gives, I certainly do not claim to be an expert on mental health. Nor do I claim that my experiences are normative. We're all different. But the subject matter makes this uniquely exposing.

So what I do know is that it will not do my equilibrium any good at all to become a counsellor to every reader. So please don't expect that. That is part of the reason for providing links to various online options.

This does not mean that I never want to hear from you! My primary concern in all this is that this provides the sense of friendship that I felt with reading William Styron. I would love to have been able just to tell him how much his book mattered to me. If there has been a resonance or connection at any point, then for that I rejoice. This is where I chime completely with Elizabeth Wurtzel's longing: 'That is all I want in life: for this pain to seem purposeful.'[1]

NOTES

## Introduction

1. Langham Partnership was formed to bring the key legacy
   ministries of John Stott under one umbrella, and was named
   after All Souls, Langham Place, where John had been Rector
   and then Rector Emeritus between 1950 and his death in 2011.
   Although there are good friendships between the church
   and organization, they are completely independent of each
   other.

## 1. The mask

1. *A Wilderness of Mirrors: Trusting Again in a Cynical World*
   (Zondervan, 2015).
2. United Nations High Commissioner for Refugees, also known
   as the UN Refugee Agency.
3. This was a hate speech bill, and with great irony, it would not
   have been defeated had the then Prime Minister Tony Blair been
   asked to stay in the building to vote – instead, his chief whip
   thought they had the vote secure and told him that he could go
   home for the night.

4. One of the greatest films ever made (in my view!), *The Lives of Others* (or in its German original, *Das Leben der Anderen*), revolves around the impact on a senior Stasi officer of surveilling a playwright and his lover. All the Stasi scenes were filmed in their correct locations.

## 2. The volcano

1. William Styron, *Darkness Visible: A Memoir of Madness* (Vintage Classics, 2001 edn).
2. Most notable are *If This Is a Man* and *The Truce*. His passion for chemistry is conveyed in *The Periodic Table*, which has been hailed as one of the greatest science books ever written.
3. For Wiesel's original Italian, see Elie Wiesel, 'Con l'incubo che tutto sia accaduto invano', *La Stampa*, Turin, 14 April 1987, p. 3.
4. In particular, Andrew Solomon (who wrote another important book on depression, *The Noonday Demon*, Vintage, 2002) has spoken powerfully about why Styron's book is so significant: <www.npr.org/2014/12/17/371364727/25-years-ago-darkness-visible-broke-ground-detailing-depression>.
5. Styron, *Darkness Visible*, p. 5.
6. Ibid., p. 14.
7. Ibid., p. 37.
8. Ibid., p. 49.
9. Matt Haig describes this sensation well in his excellent *Reasons to Stay Alive* (Canongate, 2015).

## 3. The cave

1. John Bunyan, *The Pilgrim's Progress* (Moody Press, 2007), p. 152.
2. Matthew Johnstone, *I Had a Black Dog* (Robinson, 2007), and *Living with a Black Dog* (Robinson, 2008).
3. Robert Southey, *The Life and Works of William Cowper* (Andesite Press, 2017), p. 137.

4. C. S. Lewis, *The Four Loves* (William Collins, 2016), p. 103.

5. Ibid., p. 65.

## 4. The weight

1. 'A General Confession', *The Book of Common Prayer* (1928).

2. 'Grace', from *All That You Can't Leave Behind* (2000), lyrics by Bono, music by U2.

3. Philip Yancey, *What's So Amazing about Grace?* (Zondervan, 1997), p. 45.

4. John Bunyan, *The Pilgrim's Progress* (Moody Press, 2007), p. 51.

## 5. The invisibility cloak

1. I explore these issues in greater depth in my essay, 'You Carried My Cross of Shame – from crippling stigma to infectious joy in the songs of U2', in the anthology *Take Me Higher: U2 and the Religious Impulse*, ed. Scott Calhoun (Bloomsbury, 2018).

2. To be found in her anthropological study of Japan in *The Chrysanthemum and the Sword: Patterns of Japanese Culture* (Houghton Mifflin, 1946).

3. John Forrester, *Grace for Shame: The Forgotten Gospel* (Pastor's Attic Press, 2010), pp. 23–24.

4. *Iliad*, 24:45–54, translation by Kenneth Dover, in Kenneth J. Dover and Christopher Burstall, *The Greeks* (BBC Publishing, 1980), p. 73.

5. Glynn Harrison, *The Big Ego Trip* (IVP, 2013), pp. 141–142, original emphasis.

6. Curt Thompson, *The Soul of Shame: Retelling the Stories We Believe about Ourselves* (IVP USA, 2015), p. 24.

7. Nick Duffell, *The Making of Them: The British Attitude to Children and the Boarding School System* (Lone Arrow Press, 2010), p. 10.

8. Thompson, *The Soul of Shame*, p. 10.

9. Timothy Keller, with Kathy Keller, *The Meaning of Marriage: Facing the Complexities of Commitment with the Wisdom of God* (Hodder & Stoughton, 2011), p. 95.

10. Charles Wesley, 'And Can It Be' (1738).

11. John Forrester, *Grace for Shame*, p. 152.

## 6. The closing

1. William Butler Yeats, 'Aedh Wishes for the Cloths of Heaven' (1899).

2. <www.iasp.info/> (accessed 9 January 2017).

3. Figures taken from <www.samaritans.org/about-us/our-research/facts-and-figures-about-suicide> (accessed 9 January 2017).

4. At the end of J. R. R. Tolkien's *The Return of the King*.

5. This verse is the inspiration for the classic work of Puritan pastoral writing, *The Bruised Reed*, by Richard Sibbes – if one can overlook the book's persistent anti-Catholic rhetoric that was typical of the era, it is truly balm for the soul!

6. See the footnote in the ESV translation.

7. <www.thegospelcoalition.org/article/why-pastors-are-committing-suicide> (accessed 27 November 2016).

8. Mike Ferry <www.huffingtonpost.com/mike-ferry/sensory-deprivation-tanks_b_7041412.html> (accessed 19 January 2017).

9. Kathryn Greene-McCreight, *Darkness Is My Only Companion* (Brazos Press, 2015), p. 15.

10. U2, 'Wake Up Dead Man' (*Pop*, 1997), words and music by Adam Clayton, Dave Evans, Larry Mullen, and Paul Hewson.

## Interlude

1. Andrew Peterson, 'The Rain Keeps Falling', © 2015 Jakedog Music/Music Services (Adm Song solutions <www.songsolutions.org>). All rights reserved. Used by permission.

## 7. The Way

1. See 1 Samuel 21:10–14 for background.

2. In his commentary on the parable of the vineyard labourers (Matthew 20:1–16).

3. I have explored the problem extensively in both *A Wilderness of Mirrors* (Zondervan, 2015), especially ch. 6, and more briefly in *What Makes Us Human?* (The Good Book Company, 2015), ch. 1.

4. C. S. Lewis, *A Grief Observed* (HarperCollins, 2012), p. 6.

5. Ibid., p. 1.

6. Ibid., p. 59.

7. Ibid., p. 76.

8. Anselm's original Latin was *fides quaerens intellectum*, from which comes my blog's rather pretentious Latin title, Quaerentia!

## 8. The fellow-travellers

1. Suzanne Collins, *Mockingjay* (Scholastic, 2010), p. 353.

2. C. S. Lewis, *The Problem of Pain* (HarperOne, 2001), p. 161.

3. Information supplied by <https://en.wikipedia.org/wiki/Magical_creatures_in_Harry_Potter#Dementors>.

4. As quoted on <www.telegraph.co.uk/men/thinking-man/stephen-frys-best-quotes/stephen-fry-quotes17> (accessed 27 October 2017).

5. John Bunyan, *The Pilgrim's Progress* (Moody Press, 2007), p. 158.

## 9. The gift

1. Sandra Newman and Howard Mittelmark, *How Not to Write a Novel* (Penguin, 2009), p. 15.

2. Malcolm Guite, *The Word in the Wilderness: A Poem a Day for Lent and Easter* (Canterbury Press, 2014), p. 8.

3. Zack Eswine, *Sensing Jesus* (Crossway, 2013), p. 135.

## Appendix 1: Managing the symptoms

1. Arthur Bennett, *The Valley of Vision: A Collection of Puritan Prayers and Devotions* (Banner of Truth, 2002).
2. Douglas Kaine McKelvey, *Every Moment Holy* (Rabbit Room Press, 2017).

## A small closing word of caution

1. Elizabeth Wurtzel, *Prozac Nation: Young and Depressed in America* (Houghton Mifflin Harcourt, 2014), p. 30.